READING

Aspirations

Remember to think about

- What has helped me learn effectively today?

- What strategies could I use to progress further?

- In what other subjects could I apply these skills?

- When could I use these skills outside of school?

Badger Publishing

Badger Publishing Limited
15 Wedgwood Gate
Pin Green Industrial Estate
Stevenage, Hertfordshire SG1 4SU
Telephone: 01438 356907   Fax: 01438 747015
www.badger-publishing.co.uk
enquiries@badger-publishing.co.uk

Badger KS3 English
Aspirations • Reading

First published 2009
ISBN 978-1-84691-457-7

Text © Jonathan Morgan 2009
Complete work © Badger Publishing Limited 2009

Acknowledgements
With thanks to the following for permission to reproduce
the following copyright materials: BBC (website), The
Poetry Archive (UK), The British Army, Penguin Books Ltd,
Shelter, Barnardo's, Paul Whkan, The Mirror (newspaper),
The Sun (newspaper) The British Red Cross, The Observer
(newspaper), The UK Youth Parliament

Efforts to contact other copyright holders have
proved unsuccessful. If any of them would care to contact
Badger Publishing Limited, we will be happy
to make appropriate arrangements.

Publisher: David Jamieson
Editor: Danny Pearson
Designer: Fiona Grant
Cover Photo: Getty Images

Printed and bound in China through Colorcraft Limited, Hong Kong

Aspirations — Reading contents

Introduction

How can I improve through using this book?

The aims of this book are to develop your reading skills to enable you to be an active and critical reader. Each chapter will consist of a range of challenges which should support your journey to become a more effective reader.

How is it organised?

Each chapter will consist of a range of challenges which will develop your

- Thinking Skills
- Ability to communicate effectively to support your reading
- Knowledge of how to succeed (what good looks like)
- Understanding of what stage of learning you are at, and how best to progress
- Awareness of how you can apply your skills to other subjects and the outside world

There is also a section in each chapter (Personalised Progression) in which you will be able to reflect on what level you are working and get advice on how to move to the next level.

What topics will I be studying?

You will be asked to analyse three texts which will be linked through a common theme or subject matter. In the following chapters, you will be looking at the following issues:

Chapter 2 Going over the top?

Chapter 3 It beggars belief.

Chapter 4 Deadly Disasters

Chapter 5 The rise of yob culture or mis-understood youth?

Chapter 6 Detonating the sound and fury

Approaching a reading text

When approaching a reading text, particularly if you have not seen it before, it is important to consider the following:

Producer	• Who has written this? - company/individual
Purpose	• Why has it been written? To discuss an issue/ entertain/shock/inform/persuade?
Audience	• Who has it been written for – age/beliefs/social groupings? • Intended effect on the reader. How does it make you feel? Indifferent/amused/entertained/ shocked/guilty/sympathetic/angry. • Has it changed your views on an issue?
Language	• What type of words are used? (*informal/formal/colloquial/persuasive*) • Comment on the sentence structure – length, variation in pace, rhetorical questions etc.
Layout/structure	• What are the methods of presentation? columns/sub-headings, photographs, captions, logos, slogans etc.
Personal Response	• How effective is the article in achieving it purpose? • What could have been improved?

How to respond to a reading question

How does the writer create the impression that James is dreading school?

James walked slowly, thoughtfully, almost trance like through the prison gates - St. Mark's Roman Catholic School etched treacherously along the arched dome, piercing his saucer eyes.

Suddenly, fear surrounded him, holding him ransom, like a hostage approaching his first day captive. As he shuffled towards the chains, a blurred image of hope waved at him, through the murky future ahead.

"You're James aren't you?"

It was Michelle, the girl he thought he'd lost to St Elizabeth's and here she was loosening the chains, and releasing him from his lonely lighthouse.

Pupil response:

The movement of James 'slowly, methodically, trance like' as well as the comparison of the school to be like a prison and a globe, gives the impression that James is terrified and anxious about the prospect of going to school.

Notice how the pupil has covered the main aspects of the question, used evidence carefully and explained the points made.

Understanding a writer's toolbox.

When responding to a reading question it is important to:

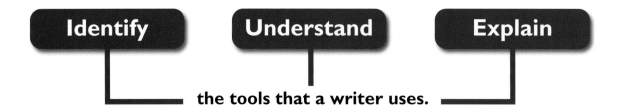

Identify   **Understand**   **Explain**

the tools that a writer uses.

Inside the writer's toolbox.

- Sentence structure – short/long/beginning with the emotions or dramatic verbs/ effective use of punctuation etc.
- Varied vocabulary
- Use of persuasive/emotive/dynamic language
- Use of senses
- Use of imagery
- Comparisons
- Repetition
- Contrast
- Personification
- Hooking devices

Connecting with a text
What should I do whilst I read?

Being an effective reader involves many skills, many which we do automatically. For example, when you read the following passage, what questions are you asking of the text?

> My wrists were handcuffed behind my back, and a black hood had been pulled down over my head. And as I sat there - in danger, and afraid - I had a great sense of being at the very lowest point of my life.

Effective reading strategies

Think about whether you did any of the following

- Hear a voice
- See images
- Speculate/ ask questions/ pass comment/ try to understand what is happening
- Predict what will happen
- Feel /empathise – you may feel anxious and worried for the victim
- Form a point of view (on the events/characters)

It is important that as you read a text that you establish a connection with the author and the characters within it so that you are beginning to form an opinion of what the text is about and what techniques the writer is using to achieve the effects that are created on you. Sophisticated readers begin forming a point of view on the events that unfold and also question the motives of the author in producing the text.

The key questions to ask when reading any text are:

- **Who has produced this text and what might this tell me about their agenda? (individual author/company)**

- **What is it trying to achieve? (purpose)**

- **How does it try and achieve this? (layout and language features)**

- **How does it want me to respond? (intended effect on reader)**

- **How do I actually respond? (consider your personal response through evaluating its impact)**

Using active reading strategies effectively

It is important that during the reading process you actively become engaged with the text and develop a personal response to the events and characters. Below are some examples of the type of responses you can make when actively reading.

Hear a voice
Quickly realise that it is from the point of view of someone who is suffering and in danger.

See images
The handcuffs/the black hood – trying to visualise what the people involved look like.

> The kidnappers had forced me to lie face down on the floor. But after they left, and the small, bare room had fallen silent, I rolled over and pulled myself slowly into a sitting position. My wrists were handcuffed behind my back, and a black hood had been pulled down over my head. And as I sat there - in danger, and afraid - I had a great sense of being at the very lowest point of my life.

Predict what will happen
Could he be killed?
Will he escape?

Feel /empathise – you may feel anxious and worried for the victim
Just imagine how much fear he is feeling. I wish I could get him out of there.

Form a point of view (on the events/characters)
If he wants to put his life in danger, that's his problem. We never should have gone to war in Iraq.

Speculate/ ask questions/ pass comment/ try to understand what is happening
Who is being handcuffed? Who is the criminal here? Where are they? Why is this taking place?

Programme of Study Links	**Creativity** - Making fresh connections between ideas, experiences, texts and words.
Framework Objectives	**Reading for meaning** - Understanding and responding to print, electronic and multi-modal texts. Analysing writers' use of organisation, structure, layout and presentation.
Thinking Skills	**Enquiry** - predicting outcomes **Creative** - Apply imagination **Information processing** - Sort and classify
AFL	Peer assessment Writing own success criteria Reflecting on the learning process
Assessment Focus	**AF4:** understand, describe, select or retrieve information, events or ideas from texts and use quotation and reference to text.
Functional Skills	Responding to junk mail as a critical reader

Challenge 1 - Get thinking

a) In pairs, look through the images below and consider the following prompts for discussion:

b) Select the three images which you feel most effectively sum up the story
c) Think of an effective headline or caption for one of these images.
d) Explain your decisions to your talk partner.

What has helped me learn effectively today?

Below is an overview of how you will develop your skills as an effective and critical reader in this unit.

In this unit I will learn how to effectively... *(Learning Objectives)*	• Extract the main points from a text • Use inference and deduction • Make notes • Analyse the structure and layout of a text
The topics I will be studying are... *(Stimulus)*	**Representations of War** • BBC News Web-page • Veteran poem • British Army website
My understand will be checked by seeing how I... *(Assessment Criteria)*	• Understand, describe, select or retrieve information, events or ideas from texts and use quotation and references to the text. (AF2)
My achievement will be demonstrated through me successfully completing the following challenges: *(Learning Outcomes)*	1. Get thinking (image) 2. Connecting with the text 3. Apply your skills – paragraph 4. Create your own success criteria 5. Get thinking verb task 6. First impressions 7. Apply your skills – inference & deduction 8. Success criteria – question/answer 9. Get thinking – Ranking task 10. Making notes 11. Apply your skills – persuasive analysis 12. Success criteria – stages of learning 13. Future skills 14. Progress challenge (AF2)

As you read the following text, remember to use the reading strategies (from Chapter 1) so that when you are at the stage of closer reading and analysis you have already made a connection with the text to inform your understanding.

ALAN JOHNSTON: My kidnap ordeal

As he neared the end of a posting in Gaza, the BBC's Alan Johnston was seized at gunpoint by militants. Here he tells the full story of his 114 days as a hostage.

The kidnappers had forced me to lie face down on the floor. But after they left, and the small, bare room had fallen silent, I rolled over and pulled myself slowly into a sitting position.

My wrists were handcuffed behind my back, and a black hood had been pulled down over my head. And as I sat there - in danger, and afraid - I had a great sense of being at the very lowest point of my life.

The Jihadi leader

He stepped into the room and sat down heavily in a white plastic chair. "Alan Johnston," he said in English. "We know everything." He said that my kidnapping was about securing the release of Muslims jailed in Britain. Crucially, he said that I would eventually be allowed to leave. I asked when, but he just said, "When the time is right."

Did he mean weeks, or months, or longer? It was impossible to say. I did fall asleep again, but I was woken by two men coming into the room. They handcuffed me and put the black hood back over my head, and led me slowly out into the cold of the night. There was no word of explanation, and as my mind searched for one in that terrifying moment of uncertainty, I feared, as I walked into the darkness, that I might be going to my death. That I was being taken somewhere to be shot.

My first cell

In this blurred, empty room I began to try to come to terms with the disaster that had engulfed me. I paced backwards and forwards across the cell. Five strides, then a turn, and five strides back. Mile, after mile, after mile. Imagine yourself in that room. Imagine pacing, or just sitting for three hours, for five hours, for 10 hours. After you had done 12 hours, you would still have four or five more before you could hope to fall asleep. And you would know that the next day would be the same, and the next, and the one after that, and so on, and on, and on.

Report of my death

In those first, terrible days - the hardest that I have ever known - I worried very much about the impact my abduction would have on my elderly parents and my sister at home in Scotland.

"After worrying about them so much it was a vast relief to see my father make a powerful and dignified address"

في حالة تَم مهاجمة مكاني , وقد أخبروني أن المكان الذي أختبئ به سيتحول إلى - منطقة موت - في حال تم محاولة

One of my lowest moments came during a power cut. I lay in a dwindling pool of candlelight, listening to the shouting, rowing neighbours and occasional gunshots that are all part of the noisy clamour of Gaza's poorer neighbourhoods. I felt very, very far from home, trapped, and aghast at how dire my situation was. Things were, however, just about to get a little better.

Desperate for some distraction to ease the psychological pressure, I had repeatedly asked for a radio, and amazingly, on the night of that power cut, a guard brought one into my room. Suddenly I had a link with the outside world. A voice in my cell, and something to listen to other than my own frightening thoughts.

And through the radio I became aware of the extraordinary, worldwide campaign that the BBC was mobilising on my behalf. It was an enormous psychological boost. But the radio also brought dreadful news. In those calm, measured tones of the BBC,

I heard reports of a claim that I had been executed. It was a shocking moment. I had been declared dead.

And I thought how appalling it was that my family should have to endure that. I was sure that if I was to be put to death, the act would be video-taped in the style of Jihadi executions in Iraq.

Threat to kill me

A few weeks later my guard barged into my room with a set of manacles. My wrists and ankles were chained together. And the guard shut my window, and put off the light, leaving me in the dark to swelter in Gaza's summer heat. He told me that it was being decided whether I should be put to death in the days ahead. If that was to happen, he said, my throat would be cut with a knife.

I did not quite believe the threat, but again, I had to prepare myself for the worst. But mercifully, the crisis passed. In fact, the chains came off after just 24 hours, and as the days went by, the threat of execution seemed to recede again.

Terrifying ride

A hood was put over my head, and I was led stumbling out into the darkness as members of the gang began to hit me and slam me against walls and the side of a car, before I was shoved into its back seat. The kidnappers and the powerful clan that was protecting them, seemed to have buckled under the Hamas pressure. They had agreed to deliver me up, in return for their survival.

But I did not know that, as the car began to move slowly towards the Hamas lines - and the most terrifying ride of my life began. Khamees struck at my head, and I could taste blood in my mouth.

At one of the checkpoints, through the wool of my mask, I could see the muzzle of a rifle inches from my eye and I knew that the guard on my right was roaring that he would put a bullet in my brain if the Hamas men did not back off. In the extraordinary tension and the confusion it seemed that a gun battle might erupt at any moment and the car would be filled with bullets.

I'm going to be fine

Eventually we came to a halt, and Khamees dragged me out into the road. I looked up to see the alleyway filled with armed men standing in the street light. Two of them stepped forward and led me away. I was afraid that this was some new gang to which I had now been passed on. But actually these were Hamas men, and as we turned a corner, there, standing in a garden, was my old friend and colleague, Fayed Abu Shamalla of the BBC Arabic service.

Alan's friend Fayed Abu Shamalla

Only then did I know that my kidnap was over, and that I was free. Days later, I was back in Scotland, taking that road that I know so well - heading at last for the hills of Argyll, and my family. But the experience of incarceration does have a way of lingering, of haunting the nights.

And the kidnap's legacy is not all bad. With its locks and chains, its solitary confinement and moments of terror, it was a kind of dark education. Even now, more than three months after I was freed, it can still seem faintly magical to do the simplest things, like walk down a street in the sunshine, or sit in a café with a newspaper. And in my captivity in Gaza, I learnt again that oldest of lessons. That in life, all that really, really matters, are the people you love.

Alan returned to the Uk on July 7

Extracting the main points from a text

What reading strategies can I use to help me understand a text?

a) skimming   b) scanning

Skimming

Getting a sense of what the whole text is about through glancing over the whole piece of information and looking for clues to help establish:

> **Text type** – What is it? A diary/website/poem etc.
> **Author** – Who has produced this text?
> **Purpose** – What is it trying to achieve?
> **Audience** – Who is it aimed at?

Once you have established this, you can then closely read the text in an informed way to develop a greater understanding. Below is the beginning of the article you have just read. Notice how quickly it is possible to establish the text type, author, purpose and audience simply by skimming the opening of the text and picking out clues (highlighted).

BBC NEWS ▶ LIVE   BBC NEWS CHANNEL

**ALAN JOHNSTON:
My kidnap ordeal**

As he neared the end of a posting in Gaza, the BBC's Alan Johnston was seized at gunpoint by militants. Here he tells the full story of his 114 days as a hostage.

Text type – Website – shown through the overall web layout use of 'LIVE'.

Author – BBC reporter Alan Johnson – use of word 'My' tells us it is his personal story. Also 'From our own correspondent'

Purpose – To inform the reader about the ordeal of being captured and to help the writer in dealing with such a terrible event

Audience – People interested in politics/current affairs/BBC website viewers

Scanning

Finding a particular piece of information for analysis.

For this type of question, we need to search for specific parts of the text in order to retrieve information. For example:

> Find two examples of how Alan Johnston was physically treated when the Jihadi leader arrived.

Before you begin looking through the whole text again, it is important to look for the clues in the question as well as the text. In this instance, the key words in the question are highlighted below:

> **Find two** examples of how Alan Johnston was **physically treated** when the **Jihadi leader** arrived.

- **Jihadi leader** – *scan the text to find references to this*
- *Simply **find** and record **two** examples – no need to explain*
- *Only look for examples of **physical** abuse – not his feelings*

You will see below that a paragraph is titled in bold **The Jihadi leader** therefore that is the only place you need to focus your reading on for this question. A reading question will often direct you to a particular paragraph number therefore it is important to number each paragraph during your first read. As you scan this passage, you will notice that two examples of physical treatment have been highlighted.

The Jihadi leader
He stepped into the room and sat down heavily in a white plastic chair. "Alan Johnston," he said in English. "We know everything."
He said that my kidnapping was about securing the release of Muslims jailed in Britain. Crucially, he said that I would eventually be allowed to leave. I asked when, but he just said, "When the time is right." Did he mean weeks, or months, or longer? It was impossible to say. I did fall asleep again, but I was woken by two men coming into the room. They handcuffed me and put the black hood back over my head, and led me slowly out into the cold of the night. There was no word of explanation, and as my mind searched for one in that terrifying moment of uncertainty, I feared, as I walked into the darkness, that I might be going to my death. That I was being taken somewhere to be shot.

Therefore, your answer should simply read:

1) Handcuffed   2) Black hood put over head
You were only asked to find, therefore you only need to retrieve the information, rather than explain it in detail.

Using the paragraph below, independently complete the following question:

a) Pick out one example which best describes Alan's feelings as he listened to the gun shots of Gaza.

> **I lay in a dwindling pool of candlelight, listening to the shouting, rowing neighbours and occasional gunshots that are all part of the noisy clamour of Gaza's poorer neighbourhoods. I felt very, very far from home, trapped, and aghast at how dire my situation was. Things were, however, just about to get a little better.**

Challenge 4 - Creating your own success criteria

When could I use these skills outside of school?

What is success criteria?

This is basically the ingredients of success - what 'good' looks like. For this challenge you will be finding out for yourself what a good response looks like, before applying it to a set of questions that you will be producing.

With your work partner, consider what questions would help pupils to understand the text more fully. In this unit, you are being tested on AF2 (understand, describe, select or retrieve information, events or ideas from texts and use quotation and reference to the text) therefore you will need to choose questions which ask pupils to find and record important information.

a) Firstly, choose 5 questions each, - using some of the sentence starters below:
- Pick out…
- Write down…
- Find…
- Give an example of…
- Identify…
- List…

b) Narrow down your 10 choices to what you think are the best 5 questions (questions which will help students understand the text fully)

c) Decide on what answers you will accept as correct. For example:

What was Alan worried about during his first few days?

Will accept: parents/sister

Wont accept: himself/dying

d) Swap questions with other pairs and complete the questions set.

e) Once the questions have been completed, mark each question, using the criteria you have come up with.

a) With your work partner, use the following list of verbs to create an image of war.

* *shudders* * *dragging* * *shattered* * *beating* * *melted* * *buries*

b) Swap your image with another group and label the picture, using these words

Using inference and deduction to understand layers of meaning

What is inference?

The skill of interpreting a text which goes beyond the literal information given to you.

What is deduction?

Understanding which is based on the evidence in the text.

By using inference and deduction you are making a connection with the text, the author's intentions and considering the impact on you as a reader.

For example:

> **Terry finally received the coursework grade he had been pestering his favourite teacher about for over a month. At home later, when asked about his day at school, he threw his school bag at his mum before storming out, with angry tears gushing from his cheeks.**

On a literal level, *1) Terry got his coursework and 2) reacted aggressively to his mum – two separate, unrelated incidents.*

However, we can **infer** that the reason why he reacted so angrily towards his mum is because his coursework grade was not what he had hoped for. In doing so, we are establishing a link with the author who has purposely left out the result of the coursework in order to engage the reader; we are also beginning to form a relationship with Terry, who we are unlikely to feel angry towards (despite his reaction towards his seemingly innocent mum) and may begin to feel sympathy and understanding for his situation.

Using active reading strategies effectively

On the next page is a poem by Andrew Motion in which he describes a time he discussed the second world war with his father. When reading a poem for the first time, it is vitally important that you don't try to understand all of the content and meanings on first glance; however, you do need to read with a purpose, and in particular, consider the following during your first reading:

* Who is telling the story (**the persona**) and what voices can you hear?
* Who is involved (**characters**) and how do you feel towards them?
* Where is the action occurring (**setting**) and what images can you see?
* When is it set? (**present/past**)
* What is the story of the poem (**narrative**) and how do you feel towards these events?

Veteran

Across the field, the wood
shudders under lilac cloud
which an hour ago was a bird
and is now a shroud,

draping the leafless trees
with filigree rain-gauze:
a handful of sun flukes
gilding the drab trunks.

My father and I watch:
Are we about to catch
a burst of orange afterglow,
or will the evening go

headlong down to night?
With the slow weight
Of a man dragging chains
He has managed to remain

On track through his tour
of flashbacks from the war:
three fog-soaked years
of square-bashing and canvas;

the sick, flat-bottomed dash
of D-Day; the frothy wash
of waves inside his tank
as it declined to sink;

the hell for leather advance
when the lanes of France
shrank bottle-tight, blazing;
the ash-wreck of Berlin.

This is by heart, of course,
All at his own pace
Now dust has settled again
And fear, grief, boredom, pain

Have found a way to fade
Into the later life he made.
But I still look at him –
The way his eyes take aim

And hold the wood in focus
Just in case anonymous
and twilit-baffled trees
might in fact be enemies

advancing – I look up at him
and cannot estimate the harm
still beating in his head
but hidden in his words.

What might he have done?
What might I have done
Frightened for my life
To make my future safe?

Did he kill a man?
Did he fire the gun
With this crumpled finger
Which now lifts and lingers

On the swimming glass
And points out how the mass
Of cloud above the wood
Has melted from a shroud

Into a carnival mask?
I never dare to ask.
I would rather not show
The appetite to know

How much of his own self
He shattered on my behalf.
He is my father; my father;
And from him all I gather

Are things that he allows,
Turning from the window
When in time the sky
Buries the wood entirely,

Then starting my road home
With him at liberty to dream
Through the hours before sleep
And the silences he keeps.

Andrew Motion

Before worrying about the words you are not familiar with, quickly record your first impressions with regard to the previous prompts:

- Who is telling the story (**the persona**) and what voices can you hear?
- Who is involved (**characters**) and how do you feel towards them?
- Where is the action occurring (**setting**) and what images can you see?
- When is it set? (**present/past**)
- What is the story of the poem (**narrative**) and how do you feel towards these events?

Using inference and deduction

What are the clues within this poem to help me read between the lines?

Although the phrase 'understanding the meaning' sounds complicated, in many cases a writer gives us easily identifiable clues to help our understanding.

For example, the title of the poem **Veteran** in itself suggests someone who has been in the war. This phrase is also used when describing people who are at the latter stages of their career. For example, David Beckham could be described as a veteran as he is near the end of his career.

With many poems, the clues do not always come in the first few lines, unlike a newspaper article which summarises the main action in the opening paragraph. Quite often, the meaning will become clearer as you start to make links between the stanzas; good readers will read backwards and forwards in order to make links, rather than just chronologically; they also ask questions constantly of the text in order to probe further into what the writer was intending.

Over the next two pages is an example of the type of decisions you can make as a reader when analysing a text, particularly a poem. Before this, is a glossary of some of the language which you may have found difficult to understand:

shroud	a cloth or long loose piece of clothing that is used to wrap a dead body before it is buried
drape	to drape across/on/over, etc. to put something such as cloth or a piece of clothing loosely over something:
filigree	decorative open patterns
gauze	a very thin light cloth, used to make clothing, to cover cuts and to separate solids from liquids, etc
gild	to cover the surface of something with bright golden light:
twilit	from twilight (the period just before it becomes completely dark in the evening

Actively reading

Across the field, the wood
shudders under lilac cloud
which an hour ago was a bird
and is now a shroud,

draping the leafless trees
with filigree rain-gauze:
a handful of sun flukes
gilding the drab trunks.

My father and I watch:
Are we about to catch
a burst of orange afterglow,
or will the evening go

headlong down to night?
With the slow weight
Of a man dragging chains
He has managed to remain

On track through his tour
of flashbacks from the war:
three fog-soaked years
of square-bashing and canvas;

the sick, flat-bottomed dash
of D-Day; the frothy wash
of waves inside his tank
as it declined to sink;

the hell for leather advance
when the lanes of France
shrank bottle-tight, blazing;
the ash-wreck of Berlin.

This is by heart, of course,
All at his own pace
Now dust has settled again
And fear, grief, boredom, pain

Have found a way to fade
Into the later life he made.
But I still look at him —
The way his eyes take aim

Setting seems to be a field – seems like there may be some kind of disaster occurred as the cloud is now being compared to a shroud which is associated with death, rather than a bird which is associated with beauty and life.

The vivid description of the field adds to the despondent mood – leafless/drab

Now I know who is involved. The persona is a man describing a time spent with his father when he was a boy.. The description is more positive now – burst/orange/afterglow. Is this the same place as before?

Who is this man dragging the chains? I suspect it will be the boy's father – maybe thinking about the dismal place earlier described.

Now I understand – the word flashback tells me that the father is telling the boy about his experiences in the war. That explains the two settings – the homely atmosphere is positive whereas the dismal description must have been the war.

D-day – I have heard about that in history – a famous attack in World War II. The father was obviously involved as it describes how his tank nearly sank.

He is now talking about the attack – the phrase 'ash-wreck' suggests that Berlin was in ruins. This is quite a positive description of the success enjoyed.

The tone becomes more sombre and sad here. Dust is used differently here as a metaphor for revealing his sad state of mind.
I get the feeling that his father is not content, even though the war is long over. It's as if something is missing from his life.

Actively reading

And hold the wood in focus
Just in case anonymous
and twilit-baffled trees
might in fact be enemies

advancing – I look up at him
and cannot estimate the harm
still beating in his head
but hidden in his words.

What might he have done?
What might I have done
Frightened for my life
To make my future safe?

Did he kill a man?
Did he fire the gun
With this crumpled finger
Which now lifts and lingers

On the swimming glass
And points out how the mass
Of cloud above the wood
Has melted from a shroud

Into a carnival mask?
I never dare to ask.
I would rather not show
The appetite to know

How much of his own self
He shattered on my behalf.
He is my father; my father;
And from him all I gather

Are things that he allows,
Turning from the window
When in time the sky
Buries the wood entirely,

Then starting my road home
With him at liberty to dream
Through the hours before sleep
And the silences he keeps.

I am beginning to understand that this poem is about the long term effects of the war. His father still feels frightened and on edge.

I can empathise with the man's feelings, especially as it is clear that much of his grief is being kept from the boy.

It is clear that the persona admires his father for what he has done to secure his future and put his life at risk.

The persona seems almost shocked and surprised that the father in front of him could have killed someone, especially as he uses the words such as 'crumpled' and 'melted.'

I can see that the persona is clearly close to his father's feelings here and respects him enough not to probe deeper and bring out more painful memories.

The persona clearly wishes for his father to be at peace and respects his silences whilst empathising with his deeply troubled memories which he clearly cannot shake off.

As with most poems, **Veteran** includes many examples of where you need to look beyond the literal (what has actually been written) and search for the real intentions of the poet. For this challenge, you need to consider what the meaning is beyond the actual words used. An example has been completed for you:

Example	Reading between the lines
With the slow weight Of a man dragging chains	The effects of the war feel like they are dragging him down – his painful memories are a burden which he can't shake off.
No dust has settled again	
How much of his own self He shattered on my behalf	

Challenge 8 - Create your own success criteria

In this section, we have been looking at inference and deduction and how we can read between the lines in order to understand a writer's intentions. Therefore, the questions and possible answers you come up with need to be focused on testing these specific skills in relation to the poem **Veteran**.

With your work partner, you need to:

a) produce 5 questions which would help students to understand the meaning behind the words. The beginning of these questions have been completed for you;

b) choose one quotation per question which you believe would help to support an effective answer;

c) write a good answer which integrates this quotation into the sentence.

Remember to expect the following from the questions you have produced:

Point – a focused sentence starter which addresses the question
Evidence – a carefully selected quotation
Explanation – how the quotation supports the point made
Reader – what is the intended (and actual) impact on the reader?

An example is shown below. Copy this table out and complete.

Question	P Point	E Evidence	E Explanation	R Reader
How has the boy's father been affected by the war?	It is clear that the war has had a disturbing impact on the father.	The boy's description of "fear, grief, boredom, pain"	sums up the emotions he has to deal with.	The poet wants to inform us about the long term impact of the war and we do this through empathising with the father's state of mind.
How does the reader feel when…				
Why does the poet choose to describe…				
What impressions do we get of the man's feelings when…				
Choose one line from the poem that suggests…				

Once you have written these questions, swap them with another group (without giving them your answers!) and attempt to answer their questions, using the PEER model.

a) With your work partner, read through the list of words below and rank them in the order that you think best describes someone who wants to join the army. (1=best described 10 = least described)

Courageous	Foolish	Leader	Follower	Driven
Lost	Ambitious	Desperate	Independent	Dependent

b) Add 2 other qualities that you think best describes someone who wants to join the army.

c) Write 2 sentences, using these lists of words 1) positive description 2) negative description.

Making notes effectively

Why should I make notes whilst reading?

- Keeps you focused
- Provides a purpose
- May stop your mind wandering
- Helps you draw out the main features of the text
- Helps you remember the information
- Provides key information which can be used when you need to write about the text
- Saves you time when asked to locate key information.

Whether it's during an exam or a task in class, you may be unable to see the question before you read the text; therefore, in order to extract the most relevant information from a text, it is vital that you make notes in a way that helps you understand and identify the

producer – (where is it from?/who is the author?)
purpose – (what is it trying to achieve?)
audience – (who is it for?)
layout features – (what presentational devices are used?)
language features – (what type of words and language devices are used?)

Once you have quickly established where it is from and what its purpose is, then the notes that you make during reading should reflect this.

For example, if the text is from the NSPCC (a children's charity organisation) it is obviously going to be a text which is attempting to inform and persuade the public; in this instance, you would be highlighting and making notes on the persuasive language and layout features.

Below is an example of how to make brief notes on a question.

1) Pick out the similes used in the passage
2) Comment on the use of personification.

You could make brief notes as shown below in order to know where to find information and evidence for each question

> **James walked slowly, thoughtfully, almost** ①
> **trance like through the prison gates – St.**
> **Mark's Roman Catholic School etched**
> **treacherously along the arched dome,**
> **piercing his saucer eyes. Suddenly, fear** ②
> **surrounded him, holding him ransom, like a** ①
> **hostage approaching his first day captive.**
> **As he shuffled towards the chains, a**
> ② **blurred image of hope waved at him,**
> **through the murky future ahead. "Your**
> **James aren't you?" It was Michelle, the girl**
> **he thought he'd lost to St Elizabeth's and**
> **here she was loosening the chains, and** ②
> **releasing him from his lonely lighthouse.**

Making more detailed notes

If you have time it is always better to include more information in your notes, which will help you understand the question. For example…

How does the writer make the reader interested in the story of the old lady?
Comment on:

> The lady's reaction to seeing the fire (1)
> Use of language (2)
> Sentence structure (3)

3) extended, complex sentences to reflect her lack of shock and relaxed, content attitude

2) use of personification to reflect feelings

1) reacts strangely which implies some involvement and lack of remorse/shock

> **Sadness loomed over her yet the clouds**
> **trickled, gently, swaying through**
> **her lighted mind. Frightened, yet no panic**
> **gripped her, it was as if she had awaited**
> **this event for a while now.**

Below are some strategies that you may wish to use in order to make notes effectively:

- Cross out the information which seems irrelevant or that is simply repeating a point previously made.
- Use an image/symbol to represent the words which seem to clearly identify the purpose.
- Change the text into a diagram in which you label the main ideas.
- Highlight words and presentational features which clearly support the purpose of the text.

- Rephrase a sentence or paragraph into one or two words.
- Use note making grids, such as the ones demonstrated below.

Examples of note making grids to use when reading a text:

Ideally, you should make your own grids which make sense to yourself, though here are some ideas:

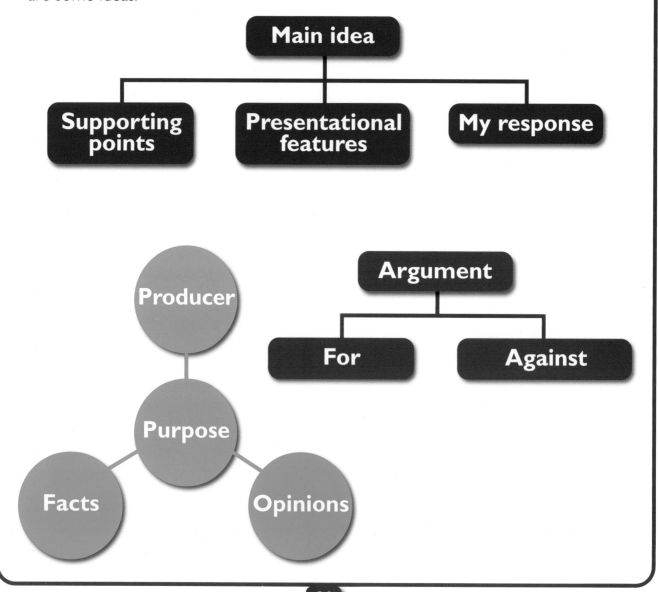

As you read the following text, make notes which relate to the following prompts:

- *Producer (Author/Organisation)*
- *Purpose*
- *Audience*
- *Presentational features*
- *Language used*
- *Impact on you as a reader — you need to put yourself into the position of being the target audience (has it achieved its purpose?)*

What strategies could I use to progress further?

www.armyjobs.mod

Tough Questions

Can I play sport in the army?

Definitely. The Army encourages all its soldiers to get involved in sporting activity both for their fitness and to build team spirit. It's a fact that many national sporting stars have served in the British Army.

How hard is soldier training?

Training isn't easy and you wouldn't expect it to be. But it is designed to get the best out of you and to help you succeed. So if you arrive in the right frame of mind you should be fine. Basic training lasts 14 weeks for adults (17-29 years old) and between 20 and 42 weeks for juniors (16-17 years old and 1 month). After basic training you progress to specialist training according to your chosen trade or job.

Will I get to travel the world in the Army?

The Army currently serves in 56 countries and if you join there's a good chance you'll get to see quite a few of them. There is also the opportunity for sponsored adventure training and sporting activities abroad.

Will I get called up?

If you are a member of the TA, you are liable for call-out under the Reserve Forces Act, 1996. This legislation was drawn up to help volunteer forces operate readily alongside Regular Forces. So if you join the TA, you indicate that you are prepared to take part in active service, whatever its nature, and there are sometimes circumstances in which you may be mobilised. However, unless the situation is extremely serious, we will usually ask for volunteers.

If you are mobilised your regular job will be legally protected. Deployment is usually preceded by a period of thorough training, which prepares volunteers for the specific military operation, whether that is a humanitarian, a peacekeeping task or a combat operation such as the recent war in Iraq.

In the event of a call-out, TA Volunteers and their employers have the right to seek exemption or deferral under certain circumstances.

Do I have to pass an entrance test?

Yes, but the test we give our soldier recruits is just our way of helping discover what types of jobs suit you best. It's known as the BARB test and includes simple maths, English and commonsense questions which are completed on a touch screen.

Army Life

Getting the most out of life is about getting the right balance, and that's what the Army provides. We'll invest time in your training, give you the space you need for your family and friends, and provide plenty of opportunities for you to learn new skills and broaden your horizons.

Making the leap from a civilian life to a military one can seem daunting at first. But in this section you'll get to meet people just like you - people who've taken the step and never looked back. You'll learn that although a role in the Army will never be easy, it is a role which, in making the hardest demands of you, will offer you true life fulfilment.

Daily Life

So what might you be getting up to on a day to day basis? Find out more about life inside and outside the Army.

Deployment and Working Overseas

International travel is a key part of Army life, giving you the opportunity to experience different places and cultures, with the full support of a team.

Initial Training

So what might you be getting up to on a day to day basis? Find out more about life inside and outside the Army.

Further Training

We never stop investing time and resources in your development. Discover some of the training opportunities that await you when you join.

Sport and Adventurous Training

Whether you're a peak-performing athlete or just looking to keep fit and meet new people, the Army offers outstanding opportunities for sport and adventurous training.

Benefits

Being in the Army is more than just a job - if you're looking to build a rewarding career then you're in the right place. With regular chances for promotion and the challenge of extra responsibility, the Army will help you fulfil your potential.

But deciding whether the Army is for you is not always an easy decision. This section aims to give you a better idea of what the Army can offer you - the challenges, the lifestyle, the job security - both now and in the future. Whatever you decide to do with your life, you're best to do it when you know the facts.

Pay, Pensions & Allowances

Find out exactly what are you going to get paid when you join the Army, now and down the track.

Time-Off & Travel

You'll get to see a lot of the world when you join the Army, both on service and in your own time. Learn about the opportunities here.

Recognised Qualifications

Find out how you can pick up valuable and recognised skills and qualifications in the Army for free.

Education & Grants

You can get a great start for life in the Army. Learn more about your educational options and the financial support available.

Family Services

Learn how the Army is there for you and your family in more ways than you've probably thought of.

Analysing writers' use of organisation, structure, layout and presentation

How does The British Army website persuade its audience to join?

Consider:

a) Who the audience are (who is it aimed at?)
b) What presentational features are used?
c) What type of language is used to achieve its aim?
d) What impact do you believe it has on its target audience (does it achieve its aim?)

Before you do this, you need make notes effectively in order to support you in this answer.

a) With your work partner, design a note making grid which will help you with finding evidence. You may wish to use some of the grids already shown.
b) Re-read the text and make notes that are concise (straight to the point) and relevant (that will help you with the questions set).
   Below is an example of how to begin this type of extended question. It is vitally important that your opening paragraph addresses the question directly and also provides a brief overview as to how you are going to organise your answer. In this way, it allows your teacher/examiner to be clear as to how you are meeting the needs of the question.

How does The British Army website persuade its audience to join?

The British Army website is clearly intending to recruit more members to the army therefore it uses a variety of techniques in order to persuade its audience that a career in the army will be a fantastic opportunity for them.

To support your answer, you may wish to use some of this list:

Presentational features	Language features
• Graphics (film scripts) • Logos • Bold • Headlines • Colour • Different font • Boxes • Pictures/photographs • Captions • Sub headings	• Use of facts and opinions • Rhetorical questions (questions that are used for effect and do not require an answer) • Emotive language • Persuasive language • Adjectives • Adverbs • Powerful verbs • Instructional language (imperatives)

With your work partner, have a brief discussion about the stages of your learning in this unit. In particular, consider the following prompts for discussion:

So what skills have I developed during this unit?

Stages of learning	What techniques did I use to progress well during this stage?	What did I find difficult? What would I do differently?	How could the task have been made easier to understand?
Challenge 9 Get thinking			
Challenge 10 Making notes			
Challenge 11 Apply your skills Extend task			

- Reading for meaning – developing active reading skills.
- Extracting the main points from a text (skimming/scanning) what has been covered.
- Understanding layers of meaning (inference and deduction).
- Making notes effectively.
- Understanding how writers organise and structure texts to impact on their target audience.

When could I use these skills outside of school?

How might I use these skills outside of school?

You receive the following letter through the post.

What would your response be to receiving this letter?

What skills are you using?

Dear Lucky Winner,

Ever fancied getting your hands on a new car or luxury holiday for free?

Well, it's your lucky day.
I am delighted to inform you that you have been personally selected to win one of our luxury prizes *.
You are guaranteed this free prize.
All you need to do is phone 08720345456 which will only cost you £1 * *

No gimmicks – no tricks – you are guaranteed to win one of our prizes.

But please hurry, this offer is only available for a short period.

Our friendly prize team are waiting to tell you about your prize.

Yours generously,
FreePrize.co.uk

* minimum prize is free entry to our prize draw
* * Phone calls £1 per minute.
Average call lasts approximately 20 minutes.

How are you addressed?

What might this tell you? (Inference and deduction)

Look for the * at the bottom of the page – what does the small print actually mean? (Skimming & scanning)

Why is the information organised as it is? (structure/organisation)

Personalised Progression

Assessment Focus 2 - Understand, describe, select or retrieve information, events or ideas from texts and use quotation and reference to text.

How is my work at KS3 assessed?

Your work is assessed using assessment focuses which help you and your teacher determine on what level your work is currently at. This criteria is used when assessing your APP work as well as your class work. In this unit we will be looking at how to progress in AF2 (see above)

Key questions:

- What level am I currently working at in this assessment focus for reading? (if unsure, ask your English teacher)
- What skills do I currently have in this assessment focus?
- What skills do I need to develop to get to the next level?

In this section, you will be completing a series of challenges which will show you how you can personally progress to the next level, using many of the skills that you have developed in this unit.

How can I practice my skills to reach the next level in this assessment focus?

- Practice skimming & scanning a text to find the correct information.
- Colour code when making notes. For example: facts/opinions/layout features/persuasive words used/adjectives/adverbs used
- List all the points you think you have made on a question and put them in rank order of most relevant to least relevant
- For each quotation you use, try to shorten it so you use only one word or phrase, rather than two or three lines for each quote.

Level 3	go to Progress Checker A (Level 3-4 progression)
Level 4	go to Progress Checker B (Level 4-5 progression)
Level 5	go to Progress Checker C (Level 5-6 progression)
Level 6	go to Progress Checker D (Level 6-7 progression)

When you get to the stage where you feel that you are confident in a particular level in this assessment focus, you can attempt the challenges for the next level.

Progress Checker A – (Level 3-4 reading progression)

Assessment Focus 2 - Understand, describe, select or retrieve information, events or ideas from texts and use quotation and reference to text.

1. What level am I currently working at in AF2 reading?	Level 3
2. What skills do I currently have in this assessment focus	As a Level 3 reader in **AF2** I am able to: • identify simple, most obvious points though I sometimes make misunderstandings • use quotations or references to the text though these are not always relevant
3. What skills do I need to develop to reach the next level?	To be a confident **AF2** reader at Level 4 I need to be more relevant when: • identifying points • using references or quotations

AF2 Progress Challenge

Moving a Level 3 response to Level 4

Remember that in order to progress to level 4 in this assessment focus you need to make your points and quotations/references more relevant to the task set.

Task:
How would you describe Alan Johnson's feelings towards his kidnap at the end of his article?

And the kidnap's legacy is not all bad. With its locks and chains, its solitary confinement and moments of terror, it was a kind of dark education. Even now, more than three months after I was freed, it can still seem faintly magical to do the simplest things, like walk down a street in the sunshine, or sit in a cafe with a newspaper. And in my captivity in Gaza, I learnt again that oldest of lessons. That in life, all that really, really matters, are the people you love.

In what other subjects could I apply these skills?

1) Put the following points and quotations in order of relevance
(1 = most relevant   3 = least relevant)

Points made

- He was pleased to be at home
- He learnt from his experiences
- He appreciates his life at home more

Quotations used

- "With its locks and chains"
- "It can seem faintly magical to do the simplest things"
- "I was back in Scotland"

1) The table below includes a Level 3 response in AF2. Look at how this pupil has achieved this level and think about what they could do to improve.

How would you describe Alan Johnson's feelings towards his kidnap at the end of his article?

AF2 – Level 3 response	Why the pupils achieved a Level 3
Alan was happy to be back home and wanted to be where people really, really loved him.	* makes simple, obvious point * makes reference to the text

How could we move this response into Level 4?

Alan was happy to be back and did want to be where people really loved him though these are very obvious statements without much reference to the text. What else could we say about Alan's feelings in the last paragraph? What quotation could we use to support this point?

AF2 – Level 3 response	AF2 – Level 4 response
Alan was happy to be back home and wanted to be where people really, really loved him.	Alan had learnt from his experiences and he calls it a "dark education"

Notice how the Level 4 response is **more relevant** to the question set even though it is shorter in length; it is more focused and also uses a direct quote which supports the point made.

Next steps… When responding to a reading question, remember to check that the points you make are directly related to the question set and the quotations you use support the point you make.

Progress Checker B – (Level 4-5 reading progression)

Assessment Focus 2 - Understand, describe, select or retrieve information, events or ideas from texts and use quotation and reference to text.

1. What level am I currently working at in AF2 reading?	Level 4
2. What skills do I currently have in this assessment focus	As a Level 4 reader in **AF2** I am able to: • identify some relevant points • use quotations or references to the text which are generally relevant though can lack focus
3. What skills do I need to develop to reach the next level?	To be a confident **AF2** reader at Level 5 I need to: • make mostly relevant points, including those selected from different places in the text. • use references or quotations that are relevant to the text

AF2 Progress Challenge B

Moving a Level 4 response to Level 5

Remember that in order to progress to level 4 in this assessment focus you need to make your points and quotations/references more relevant to the task set.

Task:
How does the British Army show that army life will be challenging and rewarding?

Army Life

Getting the most out of life is about getting the right balance, and that's what the Army provides. We'll invest time in your training, give you the space you need for your family and friends, and provide plenty of opportunities for you to learn new skills and broaden your horizons.

Making the leap from a civilian life to a military one can seem daunting at first. But in this section you'll get to meet people just like you - people who've taken the step and never looked back. You'll learn that although a role in the Army will never be easy, it is a role which, in making the hardest demands of you, will offer you true life fulfilment.

What strategies could I use to progress further?

1) Put the following points and quotations in order of relevance
   (1 = most relevant   3 = least relevant)

Points made

- It's hard though you will enjoy it.
- You make loads of new friends in the army.
- If you put the effort in you will get more out of it.

Quotations used

- "you'll get to meet people just like you"
- "we'll invest time in your training"
- "offer you true life fulfilment"

1) The table below includes a Level 4 response in AF2. Look at how this pupil has achieved this level and think about what they could do to improve.

Task:

How does the British Army show that army life will be challenging and rewarding?

AF2 – Level 4 response	Why the pupils achieved a Level 4
Army life will be really hard to get used to and you need a balance so you can enjoy it.	* point made has some relevance * reference is generally relevant though lacks focus

How could we move this response into Level 5?

This pupil is accurate in observing that army life can be hard and a balance is needed though the point made and reference lacks focus.

How else could the point be made to be more relevant?
What other quotation would more effectively answer the question?

AF2 – Level 4 response	AF2 – Level 5 response
Army life will be really hard to get used to and you need a balance so you can enjoy it.	Army life is described as being "daunting" as well as offering "life fulfilment"

Notice how the Level 5 response is **more focused** to the question set even and the quotation more effectively supports the point made

Next steps… When re-reading your AF2 responses, see if you can choose more effective quotes that more effectively link with the points you have made.

Progress Checker C – (Level 5-6 reading progression)

Assessment Focus 2 - Understand, describe, select or retrieve information, events or ideas from texts and use quotation and reference to text.

1. What level am I currently working at in AF2 reading?	Level 5
2. What skills do I currently have in this assessment focus	As a Level 5 reader in **AF2** I am able to: • make mostly relevant points, including those selected from different places in the text. • use references or quotations that are relevant to the text
3. What skills do I need to develop to reach the next level?	To be a confident **AF2** reader at Level 6 I need to: • clearly identify relevant points • summarise and combine together information from different sources • make apt textual references to support main ideas or arguments

AF2 Progress Challenge

What would you describe as the main lessons that Alan Johnson learnt from his experience?

And the kidnap's legacy is not all bad. With its locks and chains, its solitary confinement and moments of terror, it was a kind of dark education. Even now, more than three months after I was freed, it can still seem faintly magical to do the simplest things, like walk down a street in the sunshine, or sit in a cafe with a newspaper. And in my captivity in Gaza, I learnt again that oldest of lessons. That in life, all that really, really matters, are the people you love.

What has helped me learn effectively today?

In order to achieve a level 6 in this response – the key aspects are

- **clearly identifying points** - not just ones that are mostly relevant;
- demonstrating the ability to **summarise and combine** information - not just select from different areas
- use of apt references that **support the main ideas** - not just points that are relevant

For example:

AF2 – Level 5 response		AF2 – Level 6 response	
Relevant points and references made from different parts in the text	*Alan was able to learn that "it can still seem faintly magical to the simplest things" and that it is "the people you love" are what matters.*	*Alan's "dark education" – the terror of his solitary confinement – has made him appreciate the "simplest things" in life.*	Summarising and combining points Apt textual references to support main idea.

Next steps... Practise summarising and combining quotations rather than simply selecting them. Make sure that each quote used directly supports your main idea rather than just being relevant.

Progress Checker D – (Level 6-7 reading progression)

When could I use these skills outside of school?

Assessment Focus 2 - Understand, describe, select or retrieve information, events or ideas from texts and use quotation and reference to text.

1. What level am I currently working at in AF2 reading?	Level 6
2. What skills do I currently have in this assessment focus	As a Level 6 reader in **AF2** I am able to: • clearly identify relevant points • summarise and combine together information from different sources • make apt textual references to support main ideas or arguments
3. What skills do I need to develop to reach the next level?	To be a confident **AF2** reader at Level 7 I need to: • be precise in my selection and application of textual reference to the point being made • draw on knowledge of other sources to develop or clinch an argument

Moving a Level 6 response to Level 7

Remember that in order to progress to level 7 in this assessment focus you need to:

- be precise when applying quotations/references to your points
- use other sources when developing an argument

Task: *How does the poet reveal the damaging effects of war?*

Veteran

Across the field, the wood
shudders under lilac cloud
which an hour ago was a bird
and is now a shroud,

draping the leafless trees
with filigree rain-gauze:
a handful of sun flukes
gilding the drab trunks.

My father and I watch:
Are we about to catch
a burst of orange afterglow,
or will the evening go

headlong down to night?
With the slow weight
Of a man dragging chains
He has managed to remain

On track through his tour
of flashbacks from the war:
three fog-soaked years
of square-bashing and canvas;

the sick, flat-bottomed dash
of D-Day; the frothy wash
of waves inside his tank
as it declined to sink;

the hell for leather advance
when the lanes of France
shrank bottle-tight, blazing;
the ash-wreck of Berlin.

This is by heart, of course,
All at his own pace
Now dust has settled again
And fear, grief, boredom, pain

Have found a way to fade
Into the later life he made.
But I still look at him –
The way his eyes take aim

And hold the wood in focus
Just in case anonymous
and twilit-baffled trees
might in fact be enemies

advancing – I look up at him
and cannot estimate the harm
still beating in his head
but hidden in his words.

What might he have done?
What might I have done
Frightened for my life
To make my future safe?

Did he kill a man?
Did he fire the gun
With this crumpled finger
Which now lifts and lingers

On the swimming glass
And points out how the mass
Of cloud above the wood
Has melted from a shroud

Into a carnival mask?
I never dare to ask.
I would rather not show
The appetite to know

How much of his own self
He shattered on my behalf.
He is my father; my father;
And from him all I gather

Are things that he allows,
Turning from the window
When in time the sky
Buries the wood entirely,

Then starting my road home
With him at liberty to dream
Through the hours before sleep
And the silences he keeps.

In order to be precise, it is important to select the quotations which relate most directly to the **effects** of war.

The poet describes the atmosphere of war - the field described as a shroud, the leafless trees etc; however, in terms of the effects, it is important to consider how the war has directly impacted on the boy's father. Therefore, the following references are most relevant:

With the slow weight
Of a man dragging chains

And fear, grief, boredom, pain
Have found a way to fade
Into the later life he made.

The way his eyes take aim
And hold the wood in focus

With this crumpled finger

How much of his own self
He shattered on my behalf

And the silences he keeps

Although these references have been clearly identified (Level 6) they need to be **precise** in order to reach a level 7.

How could you put these quotations into a precise explanation of the effects of war?
Look through the following paragraph and consider how the points made are precise and directly related to the effects of war.

The father's metaphorical chains reveal that he will always be affected by the war, as they drag him like a "slow weight" Moreover, as well as the physical impact "the crumpled finger" there is the emotional baggage of the "grief, boredom and pain" which explains the way his life has in many ways been shattered – resulting in the "silences" he keeps.

As well as being precise, a level 7 response should include other resources, where appropriate, when developing an argument. A resource does not necessarily need to be reference to another text – it could be a different or supporting argument. For example, in relation to this question, the other resource could be an interpretation of the impact of the war more widely. For example:

The poet reveals the deep impact of the war on those who may have survived physically though still have the emotional "chains" to carry round. Perhaps he wishes to tell the often untold story of those who do not get the dramatic headlines though are still feeling the consequences years later – consequences which have clearly been passed on through generations.

You will notice here that this response demonstrates wider knowledge of the topic and relates this knowledge (resource) into the context of the question.

In order to be precise, it is important to select the quotations which relate most directly to the effects of war

The poet describes the atmosphere of war - the field described as a shroud, the leafless trees etc. However, in terms of the effects, it is important to consider how the war has directly impacted on the boy's father. Therefore, the following references are most relevant:

With the slow weight *Of a man dragging chains* *And fear, grief, boredom, pain* *Have found a way to fade* *Into the later life he made.*	*The way his eyes take aim* *And hold the wood in focus* *With this crumpled finger* *How much of his own self* *He shattered on my behalf* *And the silences he keeps*

Although these references have been clearly identified (Level 6) they need to be precise in order to reach a level 7.

How could you put these quotations into a precise explanation of the effects of war?

AF2 – Level 6	**AF2 – Level 7**
The father's metaphorical chains reveal that he will always be affected by the war, as they drag him like a "slow weight" Moreover, as well as the physical impact "the crumpled finger" there is the emotional baggage of the "grief, boredom and pain" which explains the way his life has in many ways been shattered – resulting in the "silences" he keeps	*The poet reveals the deep impact of the war on those who may have survived physically though still have the emotional "chains" to carry round. Perhaps he wishes to tell the often untold story of those who do not get the dramatic headlines though are still feeling the consequences years later – consequences which have clearly been passed on through generations.*

As well as being precise, a level 7 response should include other resources, where appropriate, when developing an argument. A resource does not necessarily need to be reference to another text – it could be a different or supporting argument. For example, in relation to this question, the other resource could be an interpretation of the impact of the war more widely.

You will notice here that this response demonstrates wider knowledge of the topic and relates this knowledge (resource) into the context of the question.

Next steps…

When re-reading your work, consider how you could include an alternative or supporting view which would help to develop your argument – this could be a personal response though make sure it is focused on supporting your argument.

Beggars Belief

Programme of Study Links	**Critical understanding** - understanding and responding to the main issues. **Cultural understanding** - exploring how ideas, experiences and values are portrayed differently.
Framework Objectives	Analysisng writers' use of organisation, structure, layout and presentation.
Personal Learning & Thinking Skills	Effective participators. Discussing issues of concern 'homelessness'. Classification skills.
Assessment Focus	**AF4:** Identifiy and comment on the structure and organisation of texts, including grammatical and presentational features at text level.
Functional Skills	**Real context** - applying skills to conduct a debate and make links with local MP.

Challenge 1 - Get thinking

a) In pairs, discuss the following extract in relation to the prompts given
Who? Why? When? Where?

> Your pack feels like a rock under your head and your nose is cold. You wonder what time it is. Can you stop listening now, or could someone still come? Distant chimes. You strain your ears, counting. One o'clock? It can't be only one o'clock, surely? I've been here hours. Did I miss a chime?

b) Once you have completed this unit, compare your responses. How accurate were you? Were your explanations more or less imaginative than the original?

What strategies could I use to progress further?

In this unit I will learn how to effectively... *(Learning Objectives)*	(6.3) Analyse writers' use of organisation, structure, layout and presentation.
The topics I will be studying are... *(Stimulus)*	**Store Cold** - Robert Swindells **Down and Out in London and Paris** - George Orwell **Homeless leaflet** - Shelter
My understand will be checked by seeing how I... *(Assessment Criteria)*	(AF4) Identifiy and comment on the structure and organisation of texts, including grammatical and presentational features at text level.
My achievement will be demonstrated through me successfully completing the following challenges: *(Learning Outcomes)*	1. Get thinking 2. Analyse writers' tools 3. Language exploration 4. Effective sub-heading use 5. Confidence levels 6. Exploring 'street life' 7. Analysis of Orwell's language 8. Text analysis 9. 5 for the price of 1 10. Get thinking - word order 11. Persuasive methods 12. Leaflet examination 13. Future skills and Personalised Progression

In this chapter, you will develop the following reading skills:

Establishing the tools that a writer uses.

When completing any reading question effectively you will need to

- identify,
- understand   **the tools that a writer uses.**
- explain

Here are some examples of the types of tools a writer has:

- sentence structure – short/long/beginning with the emotions or dramatic verbs/effective use of punctuation etc.
- varied vocabulary
- use of persuasive/emotive/dynamic language
- use of senses
- use of imagery
- comparisons
- repetition
- contrast
- personification
- hooking devices

The following extract has been taken from a novel titled *Stone Cold* by Robert Swindells. The story follows the fortunes of 'Link' a 16-year-old boy from Bradford who becomes involved in a murderous plot in which he is the target of a homeless killer. In this passage, Link describes the harsh realities of living on the streets.

As you read the passage, consider what 'tools' are being used by Robert Swindells to create sympathy for Link's situation.

Robert Swindells – Stone Cold

If you think sleeping rough's just a matter of finding a dry spot where the fuzz won't move you on and getting your head down, you're wrong. Not your fault of course - if you've never tried it you've no way of knowing what it's like, so what I thought I'd do was sort of talk you through a typical night. That night in the Vaudeville alcove won't do, because there were two of us and it's worse if you're by yourself.

So you pick your spot. Wherever it is (unless you're in a squat or a derelict house or something) it's going to have a floor of stone, tile, concrete or brick. In other words it's going to be hard and cold. It might be a bit cramped, too - shop doorways often are. And remember, if it's winter you're going to be half frozen before you even start. Anyway you've got your place, and if you're lucky enough to have a sleeping bag you unroll it and get in.

Settled for the night? Well maybe, maybe not. Remember my first night? The Scouser? 'Course you do. He kicked me out of my bedroom and pinched my watch. Well, that sort of thing can happen any night, and there are worse things.

You could be peed on by a drunk or a dog. Happens all the time - one man's bedroom is another man's lavatory. You might be spotted by a gang of lager louts on the look out for someone to maim. That happens all the time too, and if they get carried away you can end up dead. There are the guys who like young boys, who think because you're a dosser you'll do anything for dosh, and there's the psycho who'll knife you for your pack.

So, you lie listening. You bet you do. Footsteps. Voices. Breathing, even. Doesn't help you sleep.

Then there's your bruises. What bruises? Try lying on a stone floor for half an hour. Just half an hour. You can choose any position you fancy, and you can change position as often as you like. You won't find it comfy, I can tell you. You won't sleep unless you're dead drunk or zonked on downers. And if you are, and do, you're going to wake up with bruises on hips, shoulders, elbows, ankles and knees - especially if you're a bit thin from not eating properly. And if you do that six hours a night for six nights you'll feel like you fell out of a train. Try sleeping on concrete then.

And don't forget the cold. If you've ever tried dropping off to sleep with cold feet, even in bed, you'll know it's impossible. You've got to warm up those feet, or lie awake. And in January, in a doorway, in wet trainers, it can be quite a struggle. And if you manage it, chances are you'll need to get up for a pee, and then it starts all over again.

And those are only some of the hassles. I haven't mentioned stomach cramps from hunger, headaches from the flu, toothache, fleas and lice. I haven't talked about homesickness, depression or despair. I haven't gone into how it feels to want a girl-friend when your circumstances make it virtually impossible for you to get one - how it feels to know you're a social outcast in fact, a non-person to whom every ordinary everyday activity is closed.

So. You lie on your bruises, listening. Trying to warm your feet. You curl up on your side and your hip hurts, so you stretch out on your back so your feet stay cold and the concrete hurts your heels. You force yourself to lie still for a bit, thinking that'll help you drop off, but it doesn't. Your pack feels like a rock under your head and your nose is cold. You wonder what time it is. Can you stop listening now, or could someone still come? Distant chimes. You strain your ears, counting. One o'clock? It can't be only one o'clock, surely? I've been here hours. Did I miss a chime?

What's that? Sounds like breathing. Heavy breathing, as in maniac. Lie still. Quiet. Maybe he won't see you. Listen. Is he still there? Silence now. Creeping up, perhaps. No. Relax. Jeez, my feet are cold.

Read through highlighted sections and consider how the **language devices** have been highlighted in the margins as well as the **explanation of the effect on the reader**

Challenge 2

In pairs, choose the word(s) or phrase(s) that you think most effectively support the notes made.

Use of direct, confrontational tone and personalised language **forces the reader's involvement in an uncompromising way.**

Repetition of personal pronoun 'you' **to help engage the reader and help to visualise and sympathise with Link's plight.**

Use of colloquial language **helps identify with the teenage reader.**

Varied syntax. Short, powerful sentences, **reinforces the feeling of fear and tension.**

Paragraph stands alone, **which adds more dramatic tension.**

1. If you think sleeping rough's just a matter of finding a dry spot where the fuzz won't move you on and getting your head down, you're wrong.
Not your fault of course - if you've never tried it you've no way of knowing what it's like, so what I thought I'd do was sort of talk you through a typical night. That night in the Vaudeville alcove won t do, because there were two of us and it's worse if you're by yourself.

2. So you pick your spot. Wherever it is (unless you're in a squat or a derelict house or something) it's going to have a floor of stone, tile, concrete or brick. In other words it's going to be hard and cold. It might be a bit cramped, too - shop doorways often are. And remember, if it's winter you're going to be half frozen before you even start. Anyway you've got your place, and if you're lucky enough to have a sleeping bag you unroll it and get in.

3. Settled for the night? Well maybe, maybe not. Remember my first night? The Scouser? 'Course you do. He kicked me out of my bedroom and pinched my watch. Well, that sort of thing can happen any night, and there are worse things. You could be peed on by a drunk or a dog. Happens all the time - one man's bedroom is another man's lavatory. You might be spotted by a gang of lager louts on the look out for someone to maim. That happens all the time too, and if they get carried away you can end up dead. There are the guys who like young boys, who think because you're a dosser you'll do anything for dosh, and there's the psycho who'll knife you for your pack.

4. So, you lie listening. You bet you do. Footsteps. Voices. Breathing, even. Doesn't help you sleep.

Informal tone **creates the realism**. Use of simile and final short sentence **demonstrates the disturbing and cruel nature of the streets.**

Colloquial and informal use of language, as well as the use of short and powerful sentences **helps the reader get into the mind of Link's character, therefore, heightening the tension and sympathy for his predicament.**

Variation in syntax and rhetorical questions **matches the uncertainty that Link is facing.**

Emotive, direct **appeal to the reader. Swindells is relating the character to the reader's own natural expectations from life – this helps to develop the sad and sombre mood.**

5. Then there's your bruises. What bruises? Try lying on a stone floor for half an hour. Just half an hour. You can choose any position you fancy, and you can change position as often as you like. You won't find it comfy, I can tell you. You won't sleep unless you're dead drunk or zonked on downers. And if you are, and do, you're going to wake up with bruises on hips, shoulders, elbows, ankles and knees - especially if you're a bit thin from not eating properly. And if you do that six hours a night for six nights you'll feel like you fell out of a train. Try sleeping on concrete then.

6. And don't forget the cold. If you've ever tried dropping off to sleep with cold feet, even in bed, you'll know it's impossible. You've got to warm up those feet, or lie awake. And in January, in a doorway, in wet trainers, it can be quite a struggle. And if you manage it, chances are you'll need to get up for a pee, and then it starts all over again.

7. And those are only some of the hassles. I haven't mentioned stomach cramps from hunger, headaches from the flu, toothache, fleas and lice. I haven't talked about homesickness, depression or despair. I haven't gone into how it feels to want a girl-friend when your circumstances make it virtually impossible for you to get one - how it feels to know you're a social outcast in fact, a non-person to whom every ordinary everyday activity is closed.

8. So. You lie on your bruises, listening. Trying to warm your feet. You curl up on your side and your hip hurts, so you stretch out on your back so your feet stay cold and the concrete hurts your heels. You force yourself to lie still for a bit, thinking that'll help you drop off, but it doesn't. Your pack feels like a rock under your head and your nose is cold. You wonder what time it is. Can you stop listening now, or could someone still come? Distant chimes. You strain your ears, counting. One o'clock? It can't be only one o'clock, surely? I've been here hours. Did I miss a chime?

Swap your choices with another pair and agree on which quotes most effectively support the notes made.

Text analysis

In this passage, there are a variety of techniques used by the writer to engage the reader and reveal the harsh realities of life on the street.

Typical question:

Describe the problems Link faces on the street.

P	Make point concisely, addressing the question directly.	*Link faces both physical and emotional problems through living on the streets.*
E	Use evidence.	*Link describes the "bruises on hips, shoulders, elbows, ankles and knees" as well as the "homesickness, depression and despair"*
E	Comment on the effects created	*Swindells uses emotive language and varies his sentence structure effectively.*
R	How would the reader respond?	*This creates the mood of isolation and desperation and engages the reader with Link's suffering.*

Understanding text structure and organisation

One of the main tools that a writer uses is to organise the text in a particular way in order to make the writing more effective. One of the most straightforward ways of structuring a fiction text is through the organisation of paragraphs. Writers will deliberately piece together a text, and often rearrange during early drafts so that the maximum effect is achieved.

You will notice that the highlighted extract in the previous pages had numbered paragraphs (1-8)

Challenge 4

For each paragraph, think of an effective sub-heading that sums up the main aspect of the paragraph – it could be a single word taken from the paragraph itself.

Challenge 5

Look through the questions below.

a) Consider how confident you would feel in answering these questions.

	Confident	Partly confident	Not confident
1) How does Swindell use powerful images to involve the reader?			
2) Explain whether you feel sympathy for Link from this passage. What devices has Swindells used to create the feeling of sympathy?			
3) Swindells uses a variety of sentence structures in this passage. Comment on how they are used to create the mood.			
4) How does Swindells help the reader to identify with Links' plight?			
5) Comment on what you think the writer's purpose was in revealing homelessness in this way.			

b) For the questions you feel least confident about, think about what you will need to do (who to ask/how to get the information)

c) For the questions you feel most confident about, see if you can support other people in the class (with your teacher's permission)

> "...he has merely made the mistake of choosing a trade at which it is impossible to grow rich"

a) Which 'trades' are impossible to grow rich from?

b) In pairs, list the reasons why people living on the street and begging for money should be classed as 'having an occupation'

Being a beggar is an occupation because	**Begging is not an occupation because....**

c) Keeping in the same roles, consider what words you would use to describe someone who spends their time begging on the street.

d) Think about the reasons why someone may have ended up on the street. Discuss with your work partner the following:

1) Under what circumstances would I feel sympathy for someone living on the street?

2) How would you describe your attitude towards homeless people?

3) What might make you change your perceptions?

Exploring the attitude towards homelessness in 1933

Down and Out in Paris and London by George Orwell.

The following extract was written in 1933 by George Orwell, who was concerned with the perception that the public had of homeless people, and in particular the negative publicity that they received. He spent time with the homeless of Paris and London, and here describes the social position of beggars.

As you read through the extract, consider the attitude Orwell has towards the homeless.

Don't forget to actively read.

What words and phrases does he use to reveal this attitude?

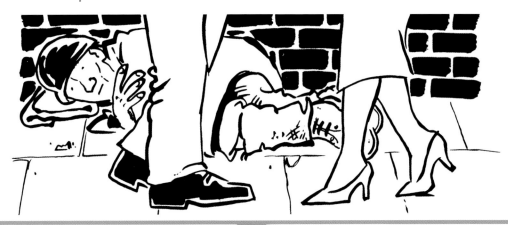

Down and Out in London and Paris

It is worth saying something about the social position of beggars, for when one has consorted with them, and found that they are ordinary human beings, one cannot help being struck by the curious attitude that society takes towards them. People seem to feel that there is some essential difference between beggars and ordinary 'working' men. They are a race apart-outcasts, like criminals and prostitutes. Working men 'work', beggars do not 'work'; they are parasites, worthless in their very nature. It is taken for granted that a beggar does not 'earn' his living, as a bricklayer or a literary critic 'earns' his. He is a mere social excrescence, tolerated because we live in a humane age, but essentially despicable.

Yet if one looks closely one sees that there is no essential difference between a beggar's livelihood and that of numberless respectable people. Beggars do not work, it is said; but, then, what is work?

A navvy works by swinging a pick. An accountant works by adding up figures.

A beggar works by standing out of doors in all weathers and getting varicose veins, chronic bronchitis, etc. It is a trade like any other; quite useless, of course-but, then, many reputable trades are quite useless. And as a social type a beggar compares well with scores of others. He is honest compared with the sellers of most patent medicines, high-minded compared with a Sunday newspaper proprietor, amiable compared with a hire-purchase tout-in short, a parasite, but a fairly harmless parasite.

He seldom extracts more than a bare living from the community, and, what should justify him according to our ethical ideas, he pays for it over and over in suffering. I do not think there is anything about a beggar that sets him in a different class from other people, or gives most modern men the right to despise him.

Then the question arises, Why are beggars despised?-for they are despised, universally. I believe it is for the simple reason that they fail to earn a decent living. In practice nobody cares whether work is useful or useless, productive or parasitic; the sole thing demanded is that it shall be profitable. In all the modem talk about energy, efficiency, social service and the rest of it, what meaning is there except 'Get money, get it legally, and get a lot of it'? Money has become the grand test of virtue. By this test beggars fail, and for this they are despised.

If one could earn even ten pounds a week at begging, it would become a respectable profession immediately. A beggar, looked at realistically, is simply a businessman, getting his living, like other businessmen, in the way that comes to hand. He has not, more than most modem people, sold his honour; he has merely made the mistake of choosing a trade at which it is impossible to grow rich.

George Orwell

In this extract, notes have been made on what the writer is intending to do (The purpose) How he manages to do this (style, use of language, rhetorical devices etc.) and what is the intended, and likely effect on the reader.

Use of impersonal, objective language suggests subtly, that Orwell's position is felt by the large majority.

Use of dramatic comparison which helps to set the beggar apart from social outcasts, helping to improve the perception of the homeless.

Use of comparison to aid argument, and persuade the reader that the beggar deserves greater status.

It is worth saying something about the social position of beggars, for when one has consorted with them, and found that they are ordinary human beings, one cannot help being struck by the curious attitude that society takes towards them. People seem to feel that there is some essential difference between beggars and ordinary 'working' men. They are a race apart — outcasts, like criminals and prostitutes. Working men 'work', beggars do not 'work'; they are parasites, worthless in their very nature. It is taken for granted that a beggar does not 'earn' his living, as a bricklayer or a literary critic 'earns' his. He is a mere social excrescence, tolerated because we live in a humane age, but essentially despicable.

Yet if one looks closely one sees that there is no essential difference between a beggar's livelihood and that of numberless respectable people. Beggars do not work, it is said; but, then, what is work? A navvy works by swinging a pick. An accountant works by adding up figures .

A beggar works by standing out of doors in all weathers and getting varicose veins, chronic bronchitis, etc. It is a trade like any other; quite useless, of course — but, then, many reputable trades are quite useless. And as a social type a beggar compares well with scores of others.

Use of 'one' implies the reader is already in agreement – a very persuasive techniques.

Cleverly dismisses and ridicules the public perception of beggars.

Uses the weaknesses of 'respected' citizens and cleverly argues that if beggars fail, then its because they do not fall victim to the greed money can bring.

Helps to sum up argument through the use of rhetorical devices.

More personal tone, using the comparison with respected professions and the despised beggars.

Use of emotive and dramatic language helps the reader to identify with the plight of the beggar.

Juxtaposition of positive adjectives with the immorality of accepted forms of employment.

Tone begins to become more defensive and assertive, pleading for a sympathetic response.

He is honest compared with the sellers of most patent medicines, high-minded compared with a Sunday newspaper proprietor, amiable compared with a hire-purchase tout — in short, a parasite, but a fairly harmless parasite.

He seldom extracts more than a bare living from the community, and, what should justify him according to our ethical ideas, he pays for it over and over in suffering. I do not think there is anything about a beggar that sets him in a different class from other people, or gives most modern men the right to despise him.

Then the question arises, Why are beggars despised? — for they are despised, universally. I believe it is for the simple reason that they fail to earn a decent living. In practice nobody cares whether work is useful or useless, productive or parasitic; the sole thing demanded is that it shall be profitable. In all the modem talk about energy, efficiency, social service and the rest of it, what meaning is there except 'Get money, get it legally, and get a lot of it'? Money has become the grand test of virtue. By this test beggars fail, and for this they are despised. If one could earn even ten pounds a week at begging, it would become a respectable profession immediately. A beggar, looked at realistically, is simply a businessman, getting his living, like other businessmen, in the way that comes to hand. He has not, more than most modem people, sold his honour; he has merely made the mistake of choosing a trade at which it is impossible to grow rich.

In this passage, you need to be clear on the following:

- Purpose – Why has this been written? What is Orwell trying to achieve by writing this extract?
- Style – How the passage has been written
- Language – The choice of words used and their dramatic effect
- Layout/Structure – How is the argument presented to the reader? Does it follow a chronological sequence or does it have a circular effect?
- Audience – Whom is he writing this for? Age/Class/Gender/ People with particular viewpoints?

Challenge 8

This is clearly a piece of argumentative and persuasive writing. We know this because of the assertive tone which Orwell uses to convince his readers that beggars should be given more respect and less criticism.

Text analysis

Using the notes made already and any of your own ideas copy out and fill in the following boxes, using evidence from the text to justify your views. Some parts have been filled in.

	Make point directly	**Evidence**
Purpose	Orwell clearly wishes to alter the perception that people have of beggars.	"Yet if one looks closely one sees that there is no essential difference between a beggar's livelihood and that of a numberless respectable people."
Style		
Language	Direct, argumentative, use of humour and satire. Use of rhetorical devices. Makes comparisons effectively.	
Layout/Structure		
Audience		

In what other subjects could I apply these skills?

Responding to an extended question

How to structure a response

How does Orwell convince his readers that homeless people deserve a better press?

Make point concisely, addressing the question directly.	Orwell challenges the idea that homeless people should be treated with less respect than 'ordinary' working men.	Point
Use evidence.	Orwell comments that beggars do work by 'standing out on doors in all weathers and getting varicose veins, chronic bronchitis etc.'	Evidence
Comment on any 'tools' used by the writer	Comparisons are drawn between the dishonest professions of a newspaper proprietor and a 'harmless' beggar. He uses emotive language and humour effectively.	Explanation
Describe the effect on the reader	The reader is engaged with the plight of the beggar through the use of emotive vocabulary and the assertive, confrontational tone of the writer.	Reader

Challenge 9 - Get 5 for the price of 1!

Using the advice above, divide into 5 groups (within the whole class) Each group is given **one** question.

1. What is the 'attitude' that society has towards beggars?
2. What comparisons are made between 'ordinary people' and beggars? Why does Orwell use these comparisons?
3. What emotive language is used by Orwell to change the reader's perceptions of beggars?
4. How does Orwell use the argument of money?
5. How successful is Orwell in achieving his purpose? Use examples from the text.

As a group, they come up with an effective answer to this question. Once completed, each group send an envoy (representative) to explain to the other groups how they responded.

What strategies could I use to progress further?

a) What is the story behind these words?

escape	**violent**	**problems**	**threatening**
cramped	**children**	**hostel**	**operation**
alone	**nightmare**	**strength**	**drained**
help	**strength**	**home**	**independent**
effective	**solve**	**control**	**trapped**
support			

b) How might you classify these words into columns? How many would you need? What would the title of each column be?

Once you have looked at the following leaflet, compare your 'story' with the original. The following leaflet has been produced by Shelter, a homeless based charity aiming to raise awareness of the plight of homeless people and gain support from the public. As you read the text, consider the methods of persuasion used by the leaflet and the intended effect on the reader.

When Sally became
homeless
she lost so much
more
than just her
home

Shelter

'It seemed like one long, terrible nightmare'

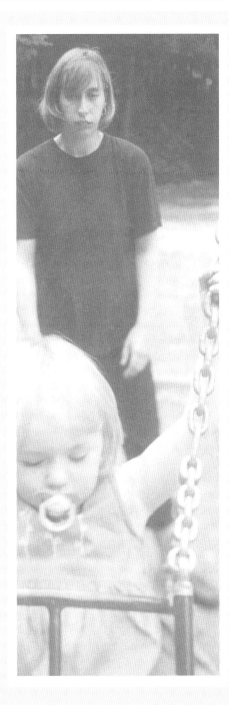

When Sally left home with her children, it was to escape her husband's violent temper.

But soon she found her problems were far from over.

For a time, she and the children lived in a small rented flat. But when her husband found her and started coming round and threatening her, she had to move again.

The next 'home' she had was in a cramped single room in a bed and breakfast where she was placed by the local council. There was hardly any room to look after two young children.

Later the council moved her to a hostel where she had to share with lots of other families. There she faced another blow – her little boy Sam, then aged three, had to have a serious operation. Far from family and friends, it was an ordeal she had to face alone. 'I used to look at Sam and think I might lose him,' she remembers. 'It seemed like one long, terrible nightmare.'

Shelter

What homeless people need most is the strength to start again

We first met Sally when one of our workers visited the hostel where she was living. Because she wasn't local, but had moved into the area to escape from her husband, the council was reluctant to re-house her. But we contacted them to press her case, and after a short period in a temporary flat she was able to move into a small terraced house.

Sally was drained emotionally by what she had been through, and didn't have a penny to spare. So we helped her move in. We provided things she needed, like pots and pans. We gave her paint and brushes to redecorate. And we continued to visit and offer practical help, such as finding Sam a place at a local school.

Sally is typical of many homeless people. She wanted so much to get back on her feet. We helped her find the strength to start again. 'I'm happy again now,' she says. 'At last I can give my kids a decent home.'

You can give homeless people what they need most – the chance to help themselves.

Shelter

What you can give to people like Sally is more valuable than money – it's the chance to help themselves

When you're homeless, money isn't what you need most. It's having someone to turn to who understands your problems, who can give you emotional and moral support, and who is there to help in very practical ways.

Every year, thousands of homeless people turn to Shelter for this kind of support. They desperately want to get back to the settled, independent life they once had. But they know they can't do it on their own.

Shelter's work is so effective because we help homeless people help themselves. We help them claim their housing rights. We can help them begin to solve the problems that led them to becoming homeless in the first place. And, through an imaginative new project called Homeless to Home, we can help them settle successfully into their new home.

That's why your support for Shelter will go much further than you may ever have thought possible to change the lives of homeless people.

Shelter

When you're homeless, there's no easy way back to a normal, settled life

As Sally found, when you lose your home you can lose a lot more besides.

Homelessness saps your morale. You lose your self-respect and can feel like a failure, even though you may be completely blameless.

Without a place of your own, you can feel that you can't control your own life. Homelessness can even take away your health. Adults and children in bed and breakfast and temporary accommodation are much more likely to suffer from asthma, bronchitis and other diseases.

What's more, homeless people often find themselves trapped in a cruel 'catch 22' situation. Without a home, they cannot get a job. Without a job, they cannot get a home.

That's why the problems of homelessness are not solved simply by giving people a roof over their heads. Often homeless people have to rebuild their whole lives – and this is where Shelter's support can be so important to them.

Your gift will make a practical difference to the lives of homeless people.

Shelter

Understanding layout, structure and organisation

In this challenge, you need to make notes in the margin on the persuasive methods used by Shelter to persuade its audience to donate money and support the homeless. Some have been completed for you.

Use of first name makes the piece more personal and therefore more appealing.

Use of dramatic, powerful adjectives to increase feeling of sympathy.

Brings children into the equation to make Sally's plight seem all the more dreadful and desperate.

Shelter

When Sally became homeless she lost so much more than just her home.

'It seemed like one long, terrible nightmare'.

When Sally left home with her children, it was to escape her husband's violent temper.

But soon she found her problems were far from over.

For a time, she and the children lived in a small rented flat. But when her husband found her and started coming round and threatening her, she had to move again.

The next 'home' she had was in a cramped single room in a bed and breakfast where she was placed by the local council. There was hardly any room to look after two young children.

Later the council moved her to a hostel where she had to share with lots of other families. There she faced another blow – her little boy Sam, then aged three, had to have a serious operation. Far from family and friends, it was an ordeal she had to face alone. 'I used to look at Sam and think I might lose him,' she remembers. 'It seemed like one long, terrible nightmare.'

What homeless people need most is the strength to start again.

We first met Sally when one of our workers visited the hostel where she was living. Because she wasn't local, but had moved into the area to escape from her husband, the council was reluctant to re-house her. But we contacted them to press her case, and after a short period in a temporary flat she was able to move into a small terraced house.

Develops sense that the organisation is worthwhile and helps the homeless properly.

Subtle, yet clever technique of suggesting the gift has already been received.

Use of personalised language 'You' to appeal directly to the reader.

Sally was drained emotionally by what she had been through, and didn't have a penny to spare.
So we helped her move in. We provided things she needed, like pots and pans. We gave her paint and brushes to redecorate. And we continued to visit and offer practical help, such as finding Sam a place at a local school.

Sally is typical of many homeless people. She wanted so much to get back on her feet. We helped her find the strength to start again. 'I'm happy again now,' she says. 'At last I can give my kids a decent home.'

You can give homeless people what they need most – the chance to help themselves.

What you can give people like Sally is more valuable than money – it's the chance to help themselves.

When you're homeless, money isn't what you need most. It's having someone to turn to who understands your problems, who can give you emotional and moral support, and who is there to help in very practical ways.

Every year, thousands of homeless people turn to Shelter for this kind of support. They desperately want to get back to the settled, independent life they once had. But they know they can't do it on their own.

Shelter's work is so effective because we help homeless people help themselves. We help them claim their housing rights. We can help them begin to solve the problems that led them to becoming homeless in the first place. And, through an imaginative new project called Homeless to Home, we can help them settle successfully into their new home.

That's why your support for Shelter will go much further than you may ever have thought possible to change the lives of homeless people.

When you're homeless, there's no easy way back to a normal, settled life.

As Sally found, when you lose your home you can lose a lot more besides.

Homelessness saps your morale. You lose your self-respect and can feel like a failure, even though you may be completely blameless.

Without a place of your own, you can feel that you can't control your own life. Homelessness can even take away your health. Adults and children in bed and breakfast and temporary accommodation are much more likely to suffer from asthma, bronchitis and other diseases.

What's more, homeless people often find themselves trapped in a cruel 'catch 22' situation. Without a home, they cannot get a job. Without a job, they cannot get a home.
That's why the problems of homelessness are not solved simply by giving people a roof over their heads. Often homeless people have to rebuild their whole lives – and this is where Shelter's support can be so important to them.

Your gift will make a practical difference to the lives of homeless people.

Challenge 12 - Detailed text analysis

For this challenge you will need to consider the persuasive devices used by Shelter to gain the public support. In particular the use of:

- Emotive language
- Facts and opinions
- Promotion of their success rate
- Direct appeal to the reader

For example:

Techniques used	Evidence	Effect on the reader
Emotive language	It seemed like one <u>long, terrible nightmare'</u>.	This helps the reader to identify with Sally's emotional plight. The use of simile is particularly effective.
Facts	The next 'home' she had was in a cramped single room in a bed and breakfast where she was placed by the local council.	Sally's plight is made realistic to the reader as we imagine the cramped conditions herself and child must have had to go through.
Promotion of their success rate	Every year, thousands of homeless people turn to Shelter for this kind of support.'	Helps to promote the organisation as a worthwhile company who have a big impact on a vast number of people. This helps to convince the reader that a donation will be very useful.'
Direct appeal to the reader	<u>Your gift</u> will make a practical difference to the lives of homeless people.	This assumes that the gift will be given; a subtle persuasive device.

There are further prompts below which should help you with this challenge

1. Pick out each example of the language that creates the impression that Sally is vulnerable.
2. How does the leaflet use presentational devices to good effect? Consider photographs, headings and logos etc.
3. How does the leaflet help to create the impression that Shelter actually works for homeless people?
4. What could a donation be used for? How might these arguments persuade its audience?
5. Is the article successful in achieving its purpose? How might it be improved?

Challenge 13 - Future skills

How might I use these skills outside of school?

As chair of your school council, you have been presented with the following issue which is affecting the local community:

In your local shopping centre, there are an increasing number of homeless people begging on the streets. They have not been causing any specific problems and the police are occasionally moving them on. Many people believe this is happening because of the amount of people losing their jobs and homes recently. However, many parents feel that it is dragging down the area and something needs to be done.

You are going to organise a debate in which school council members come up with a range of strategies to tackle this problem.

Once the debate has finished, you will present your views to your local MP in the hope of resolving this issue.

In a small group, take on the roles of:

Homeless person
Parent
Police
Shopkeeper
Pupil

Have a debate on this topic in which you consider:

a) what point of views should be expressed (with supporting arguments)
b) what you are prepared to compromise over
c) what solutions you will put forward

(remember to use some of the arguments from this chapter to inform your discussion)

Personalised Progression

Assessment Focus 4 – Identify and comment on the structure and organisation of texts, including grammatical and presentational features at text level.

How is my work at KS3 assessed?

Your work is assessed using assessment focuses which help you and your teacher determine on what level your work is currently at. This criteria is used when assessing your APP work as well as your class-work. In this unit we will be looking at how to progress in AF4 (see above).

Key questions:

- What level am I currently working at in this assessment focus for reading? (if unsure, ask your English teacher)
- What skills do I currently have in this assessment focus?
- What skills do I need to develop to get to the next level?

In this section, you will be completing a series of challenges which will show you how you can personally progress to the next level, using many of the skills that you have developed in this unit.

How can I practice my skills to reach the next level in this assessment focus?

- Number each paragraph in a text and choose a word/phrase which best sums up the main points
- Highlight the topic sentence in each paragraph
- What would be a good sub-heading for each section of the text?
- Remember that the text has been consciously pieced together for a purpose – ask yourself, why has that heading been used? Why has certain information been left out at this point?
- How do layout features used in the text add to the meaning?

In this assessment focus (AF4), if you are currently working at...

Level 3	go to Progress Checker A (Level 3-4 progression)
Level 4	go to Progress Checker B (Level 4-5 progression)
Level 5	go to Progress Checker C (Level 5-6 progression)
Level 6	go to Progress Checker D (Level 6-7 progression)

When you get to the stage where you feel that you are confident in a particular level in this assessment focus, you can attempt the challenges for the next level.

Progress Checker A (Level 3-4 reading progression)

Assessment Focus 4 – identify and comment on the structure and organisation of texts, including grammatical and presentational features at text level

1	What level am I currently working at in AF4 reading?	Level 3
2	What skills do I currently have in this assessment focus?	As a Level 3 reader in AF4 I am able to: Identify a few basic features of organisation at text level with little or no comment.
3	What skills do I need to develop to reach the next level?	To be a confident AF4 reader at Level 4 I need to identify and comment on • structural choices made • basic features of organisation at text level

AF4 Progress Challenge

For these challenges, you need to refer to the Shelter leaflet on the previous pages

Moving a Level 3 response to Level 4

Remember that in order to progress to level 4 in this assessment focus you need to make a comment on the structural choices and the way that the text is organised

1. The table below includes a Level 3 response in AF4. Look at how this pupil has achieved this level and think about what they could do to improve.

How does the organisation of the Shelter leaflet help them to communicate their viewpoints to the reader?

AF4 – Level 3 response	Why the pupils achieved a Level 3
The leaflet uses pictures because writing would be just boring.	Basic feature identified

How could we move this response into Level 4?

AF4 – Level 3 response	AF2 – Level 4 response
The leaflet uses pictures because just having writing would be boring.	*The leaflet uses pictures of Sally so we can see what her life was like.*

Notice how the Level 4 response makes a linked comment (linked in relation to the purpose of the leaflet)

Next steps…
When commenting on layout features – make a comment which links to what the purpose of the text is.

Progress Checker B – (Level 4-5 reading progression)

Assessment Focus 4 – identify and comment on the structure and organisation of texts, including grammatical and presentational features at text level	
1 What level am I currently working at in AF4 reading?	Level 4
2 What skills do I currently have in this assessment focus?	As a Level 4 reader in Af4 I am able to: • make structural choices • identify basic features of organisation at text level
3 What skills do I need to develop to reach the next level?	To be a confident AF4 reader at Level 5 I need to: • show awareness of author's craft when commenting on structural choices • clearly identify organisational features with some explanation

Moving a Level 4 response to Level 5

1. The table below includes a Level 4 response in AF4. Look at how this pupil has achieved this level and think about what they could do to improve.

AF4 – Level 4 response	Why the pupils achieved a Level 4
The leaflet uses pictures of Sally so we can see what her life was like. The sub-headings used make it clearer for us to understand.	A basic feature of organisation is identified (photograph) with a simple comment (what her life was like)

How could we move this response into Level 5?

AF4 – Level 4 response	AF4 – Level 5 response
The leaflet uses pictures of Sally so we can see what her life was like. The sub-headings used make it clearer for us to understand.	*The photographs of Sally helping out her family would encourage us to make a donation as it would make us feel that homeless people want to help themselves. The sub-heading "What homeless people need most is the strength to start again" would also encourage people to support them.*

Notice how the Level 5 response begins to explore the organisational features and how they impact on the reader

Next steps…
When commenting on organisational features, make sure that you explain how these have been used to support the author's purpose.

Progress Checker C – (Level 5-6 reading progression)

Assessment Focus 4 – identify and comment on the structure and organisation of texts, including grammatical and presentational features at text level	
1 What level am I currently working at in AF4 reading?	Level 5
2 What skills do I currently have in this assessment focus?	As a Level 5 reader in AF4 I am able to: • show awareness of author's craft when commenting on structural choices • clearly identify organisational features with some explanation
3 What skills do I need to develop to reach the next level?	To be a confident AF4 reader at Level 6 I need to include: • some detailed exploration of how structural choices support the writers' theme or purpose • comment on how a range of features relating to organisation at text level contribute to the effects achieved

AF4 Progress Challenge

In order to achieve a level 6 in this response – the key aspects are to explore structural choices and comment on a range of features that contribute to the effects.

For example:

Level 5 response at AF4	**Level 6 response at AF4**
The photographs of Sally helping out her family would encourage us to make a donation as it would make us feel that homeless people want to help themselves. The sub-heading "What homeless people need most is the strength to start again" would also encourage people to support them.	*Shelter uses structural devices such as one lined paragraphs to bring out the desperation in Sally's situation. "What homeless people need most is the strength to start again." This device encourages the reader to stand up and take notice of Sally's terrible predicament. Shelter takes you through Sally's story from being the victim of violence to becoming self-sufficient.*

Next steps… Ensure you **explore** a **range** of language features when commenting on a text and think about how the author uses these features to support the **main ideas**.

Progress Checker D (Level 6-7 reading progression)

	Assessment Focus 4 – identify and comment on the structure and organisation of texts, including grammatical and presentational features at text level	
1	What level am I currently working at in AF4 reading?	Level 6
2	What skills do I currently have in this assessment focus?	As a Level 6 reader in AF4 I am able to: • explore how structural choices support the writers' theme or purpose • comment on how a range of features relating to organisation at text level contribute to the effects achieved
3	What skills do I need to develop to reach the next level?	To be a confident AF4 reader at Level 7 I need to: • evaluate the extent to which structural choices support the writers' theme or purpose • appreciate the skill with which a range of features relating to text organisation are used

AF4 Progress Challenge

Moving a Level 6 response to Level 7

Remember that in order to progress to level 7 in this assessment focus you need to

Evaluate the use of structural choices (are they effective in impacting on the audience and enabling the author to achieve their purpose?)

Appreciate the skills used to create the range of organisational features.

For example:

Level 6 response at AF4	Level 7 response at AF4
Shelter uses structural devices such as one lined paragraphs to bring out the desperation in Sally's situation. "What homeless people need most is the strength to start again." This device encourages the reader to stand up and take notice of Sally's terrible predicament. Shelter takes you through Sally's story from being the victim of violence to becoming self-sufficient.	*The opening page of the leaflet features a despondent looking Sally, juxtaposed with the headline "When Sally became homeless she lost so much more than just her home" The disjointed text in this headline could arguably used to reflect her disjointed life. The leaflet is structured to reflect Sally's emotional journey; from being in one 'long terrible nightmare' to the strength that she has found through Shelter's help "I'm happy again now" Alongside this description is a picture in child's hand writing of a house with the words 'home, sweet home' which helps the reader to identify with the impact that Shelter can have on homeless people, particularly children.*

Next steps…

When re-reading your work, begin exploring the different effects created and whether the layout features have contributed to the overall meaning and impact on the audience.

Programme of Study Links	**Cultural understanding** - exploring how ideas, experiences and values are portrayed differently in texts from a range of cultures and traditions.
Framework Objectives	Analysisng how writers' use of linguistic and literary features, shapes and influences meaning.
Personal Learning & Thinking Skills	**Creative thinkers** - connecting their own and others' ideas and experiences in inventive ways.
AFL	Producing own success criteria through 'Millionaire' game.
Assessment Focus	**AF5:** - explain and comment on writers' use of language, including grammatical and literary features at word and text level.
Functional Skills	**Real contents that apply learning**: Volunteering opportunities/making decisions as a journalist.

Challenge 1- Get thinking

When could I use these skills outside of school?

Why it is important for us to learn about natural disasters?

1. In a group of 3 discuss what you know about the following:

- Tsunami
- Earthquake
- Cyclone

In your three, take on the following roles:

A: You express your feelings about what you know. (How people are affected by natural disasters)

B: You consider what information you will need for your presentation. (facts & figures)

C: You decide how to combine the contributions from A & B into a presentation.

By the end of this unit you will have the opportunity to include extra detail to support this presentation.

In this unit I will learn how to effectively... *(Learning Objectives)*	• analyse how writers use of language features shapes and influences meaning
The topics I will be studying are... *(Stimulus)*	**Deadly Disasters** *Tsunami* – personal account *The British Red Cross* – Cyclone appeal *China Earthquake* – newspaper article
My understand will be checked by seeing how I... *(Assessment Criteria)*	Explain and comment on writers' use of language(AF5)
My achievement will be demonstrated through me successfully completing the following challenges: *(Learning Outcomes)*	Challenge 1 Get thinking presentation Challenge 2 Antonym/adjective activity Challenge 3 Simile analysis Challenge 4 Tension graph Challenge 5 Millionaire game Challenge 6 Get thinking – article preparation Challenge 7 Earthquake analysis Challenge 8 Analysis of impact Challenge 9 Advice booklet Challenge 10 Get thinking. Image analysis/KWL Challenge 11 Summary activity Challenge 12 Persuasive language analysis Challenge 13 Sentence headline Challenge 14 Article analysis Challenge 15 Analyse the Volunteer web page Challenge 16 Future skills – Becoming a volunteer – making choices Progress Challenges

What is a Tsunami?

A **Tsunami** is a series of waves created when an ocean is displaced due to an earthquake.

On 26 December 2004 an earthquake off the coast of Indonesia triggered a massive tsunami which left nearly 230,000 people dead or missing, and another 2 million homeless.

In this passage, a survivor from the Tsunami provides a personal account of his experience. The purpose of looking at this extract is to consider how the writer uses a variety of language devices to make the event come alive for the reader. In particular, we will be looking at the use of:

Language devices	For example:
powerful verbs	Hoping the hurtling waters would not rise any farther, I thought 'Oh my God, Oh my God!', unable to think of any other prayer. But the waters were already several meters high and surging higher.
adjectives	The place was beautiful – small, quiet bungalows under the trees just next to a sweeping private and secluded beach. The air was fresh from the clean ocean air, and scented with tropical flowers
similes	my left thigh had been cut open, seemingly to the bone, with all the meat and **muscle hanging out like at a butcher shop.**

Challenge 2

Read through the list of adjectives and verbs and consider what words would act as effective opposites (antonyms) Explain your reasons to a work partner.

	Before Tsunami			After Tsunami			
Adjectives	Beautiful Private Clean Delicious	Small Secluded Tropical Peaceful	Quiet Fresh Restful				
Powerful verbs				Running Throwing Inching Yelling Watching	Hurtling Swirling Rushing Clinging Seeping	Holding Rising Hanging Screaming	Surging Floating Wailing

In what other subjects could I apply these skills?

You will notice that in the following extract, some of the adjectives and verbs from Challenge 2 have been highlighted. With your learning partner, read through the passage and:	Examples of techniques (not from article)
1. Pick out where there has been a simile used.	" her eyes danced around like blue diamonds".
2. Explain what effect it has on the reader.	This makes the reader feel that she must have been agitated or excited.
3. What other simile could you have used for it to have been even more effective.	The writer could have used "scratched blue diamonds" which would have suggested more about her state of mind.

Tsunami aftermath – a personal account
14 January 2005

The miracle was that we survived because of a sequence of lucky, providential, perhaps even fated events, any one of which could have ended our lives, or made survival that much more difficult. The area where we had been had the highest percentage of deaths in Thailand, because of the more exclusive, secluded, on the beach, low styled bungalows that were characteristic of the new area.

We had just arrived the afternoon before, flying into Phuket and driving an hour or so north to Khao Lak; the place was beautiful-small, quiet bungalows under the trees just next to a sweeping private and secluded beach. The air was fresh from the clean ocean air, and scented with tropical flowers. We had just woken up from a restful sleep, finished a delicious buffet brunch and the sky was blue with hardly a cloud in the sky; the waters were peaceful and we had just called our parents to say Merry Christmas.

A few people were walking and playing along the beach and as I walked over to the windows that looked out over a lagoon I saw a boy running as fast as he could across my field of vision, and then closely behind him a huge mass of mud brown water hurtling forward with a loud crashing sound. I felt I could scarcely hear in that thunder, feeling a strange void of sound, no screams, no cries of help, just the thundering sound of trees snapping, and the surging waters.

I hardly had time to think and could barely believe what was happening. It was so incredible, like out of a movie, or a dream. I quickly called to my girlfriend, and she jumped out of bed to stand beside me. Then we were just holding each other in a small panic. Hoping the hurtling waters would not rise any farther, I thought 'Oh my God, Oh my God!', unable to think any other prayer. But the waters were already several meters high and surging higher. The waters came up to the edge of our terrace, and then climbed up the glass doors.

My girlfriend and I backed up, jumped up onto the bed, and then there was a loud crash as the waters burst through the glass doors as if they were made of rice paper, and surged into the room, throwing everything about. We could hardly stay up on the bed, as it too was thrown back and up into the room, and then the waters were swirling about, the bed into the corner, and us on it; and then over the bed, and up to our knees, and so higher and faster. We were both in a sort of shock, it was hard to think, to do anything - not that we could, except just hold tight and try to stay upright and not get sucked into the muck. The waters were rising faster, and we were floating in it until our heads hit the ceiling, and we had eight inches of air to breathe like in the movies.

It was getting darker, and I then started telling my girlfriend and myself, we're going to die here, we're going to die here. As if preparing ourselves for the inevitable as the waters were inching higher. I was trying to remember the orientation of where the glass doors had been so we could dive under the waters and try to get out. And then we were still there at 8 inches to the ceiling for what seemed a small eternity.

In that moment when the waves first hit, and the water was rushing in, I felt pure raw fear. But it was less a fear for myself than a fear that there was nothing I could do to protect my girlfriend. Later, I saw several interviews with parents who had lost children express similar sentiments. Many had lost hold of their children as the waves took them, seeing the looks of terror on their little faces as they disappeared under the waters. And I knew some of that utterly helpless and fearful feeling.

Finally the waters started to inch down. As the waters inched below the terrace door frames, I was thinking we had to get out of here, or we would drown if another wave came. As the water receded, it started to suck everything out of the room, like the air out of an airplane if a window were to get shot out. We let ourselves drift toward the doors, thinking we might be able to get out and swim. But we held ourselves back, as the rush of the waters rushed through the open space that had been glass terrace doors.

I floated out there a few seconds trying to get a better look and assessment of what was going on, when we both realised there was no way we could swim the 100 meters or so to the halls just beyond, with the current of the water rushing around our bungalow and back out to sea. And we were hanging onto the roof, the edge of the door frame, anything to keep from getting sucked out into the rushing current.

And then the waters were halfway down the walls, and I helped my girlfriend back onto the bed, and we both realized at once that my left thigh had been cut open, seemingly to the bone, with all the meat and muscle hanging out like at a butcher shop. I felt it wasn't my leg I was looking at, I didn't even feel it. I was probably already in shock from losing blood. And my girlfriend started looking around for scraps of cloth, t-shirts, brown from the muck, to tie around my leg as a tourniquet.

We didn't hear a sound from below, but a woman in a larger house just south of us and up the hill started wailing, trying to get out. I was so glad my girlfriend kept yelling, as two young boys ran down the hill with a security officer, and I lowered her to them, her bruised arms could barely support her. Then we limped up the hill as quickly as we could. I didn't look back, but my girlfriend could see the next wave coming. As we limped up the hill, I was lucky to only pass one dead body. My girlfriend had seen several bodies clinging in the current, and washed back out to sea.

We limped up to the road, and then we could hear the screaming and wailing of people that had just made it, they had just lost loved ones, we're just starting to realise what had happened, and now we're watching as other waves were approaching. Small clumps of people by the road now started to panic and run up into the hills. We followed, barefoot, in our underwear, feeling like aboriginal natives running into the jungle. I could hardly put weight on my leg, and the blood was coming down in small spurts as my flesh split from my tourniquets with the movement.

After three weeks and three surgeries, tendons to my left foot have been reattached, and my body has fought off several strains of bacteria. My girlfriend is able to breathe again without pain, her stitches are out, and with physical therapy has regained much of her strength. In the news, and from hospital staff, I heard of horror stories of people who had relatively minor wounds, but because of neglected or complicated infections, have had to amputate limbs.
Even almost three weeks after the accident, my relatively small wounds are still seeping with fluid discharge, but the swelling has gone down, and we hope the infections are under control.
We still can hardly believe how lucky we were.

If we had been in any less sturdy of a bungalow, we could easily have been crushed, as we saw many other concrete structures crushed. If we had spent a few more minutes at brunch, or woke up a little later, we could have been on the beach when the waters came, and have been crushed again and separated by miles when the waters picked up everything in their path. If the waters had come up 8 inches higher, we would have drowned in our bungalows. If my thigh wound had been another inch or two over, my artery would have been cut, or if we couldn't get to the first hospital, I could have easily bled to death. And if we didn't get to Bangkok as quickly as we did, my wounds could have become infected leading to amputation or worse. But all that didn't happen to us.

Now still in the hospital, we are so thankful that God spared us that day. Our families and friends still cannot believe we were among the few of the lucky. And neither can we. in the local papers, we see the pictures of bodies along the beach where we were, hundreds and hundreds more in dry ice, the faces of the missing children, and we wonder about a seven year old German boy, and whether he will have to grow up without his parents.

Challenge 4 - Responding to the Tsunami account

Plotting the tension

Look at the table below and plot where the main elements of tension were. Choose one word from each stage that best reflects this level of tension

High tension						
Low tension						
	Arriving in Phukat	Boy running Sound of thunder	Waters rising and bursting through	Water inching down	On the road	Reflecting on survival

Challenge 5 - Create your own success

Who wants to be a millionaire?

Well, you wont quite win a million pounds with this challenge, though you should gain a better grasp of how a writer uses language for effect.

In a group of three, devise 5 questions in the style of *Who wants to be a millionaire?* Use the following guidance for support:

QI - £1000
Q2 - £10,000
Q3 - £100,000
Q4 - £500,000
Q5 - I million

There are 3 life lines:
1) ask the audience (the rest of class vote)
2) ask a friend
3) remove two wrong answers

Each question should get progressively harder (as in the game show). There should be a choice of four answers (the three incorrect answers should not be too obviously wrong, especially the harder questions)
Each question should be related the contestants having a greater understanding of how a writer uses language for effect. In other words, the techniques used by the author in the Tsunami article to make his experience come alive for the reader. (Don't forget to use the materials from this unit to support you)

Once you have completed these questions, play the game with the other groups in the class.

Challenge 6 - Get thinking

You have been asked to visit the scene of an earthquake and find out as much information as you can in order to write a newspaper article. Your editor is putting pressure on you to plan the report quickly for the morning's front page. Think about

1. What information you would need to get?
2. Who would you be likely to get this from?
3. What people would you like to talk to?
4. What would need to be included in your first paragraph?

For this challenge, you can either:

Work alone and record your thoughts in a format that suits you.
i.e. list/diagram
Work with a partner and discuss your views.

Once this has been completed share your thoughts with the class and complete the Challenge 7 on the next page.

1. Read through the article below on the earthquake in China. As you read through this, copy out and complete the table below.

Information I decided I would need for my article	Examples from The China earthquake

2. Consider what else you would have needed to have achieved a better outcome in Challenge 6

CHINA EARTHQUAKE: DEATH TOLL

14th May 2008

More than 50,000 people may have died in China's earthquake, the government admitted today.

Official figures put the death toll at nearly 15,000 with 26,000 still buried in rubble and 14,000 missing. As help began to arrive in some of the hardest-to-reach areas, some victims trapped for more than two days under collapsed buildings were still being pulled out alive.

But the enormous scale of the devastation meant that resources were stretched thin, and makeshift aid stations and refugee centers were springing up over a disaster area the size of Belgium.

The official Xinhua News Agency said government officials are saying rescuers who walked into the city of Yingxiu in Wenchuan county, the epicentre of Monday's magnitude 7.9 quake, found it "much worse than expected."

Confusion remained over the official figures. It was not clear if the death toll included the 7,700 reported dead in Yingxiu and whether the figures applied to only Sichuan province or included other areas where the quake struck.

The toll was expected to rise further once rescuers reach other towns in Wenchuan that remain cut off from the Sichuan provincial capital of Chengdu more than two days after the quake.

Rescuers raced to save people trapped under flattened buildings.

Roads leading to Wenchuan from all directions were still being cleared of debris. At a middle school Sichuan province's Qingchuan county where students were taking a noon nap when the quake demolished a three-story building, 178 children were confirmed dead in the rubble and another 23 remained missing.

Storms that had prevented flights to some of the worst-hit areas finally cleared and military helicopters were able to drop food, drinking water and medicine to Yingxiu. Trains were on their way to Sichuan carrying quilts, drinking water, tents and more military personnel.

A 34-year-old woman who was eight months pregnant was rescued after spending 50 hours under debris in Dujiangyan. In the Beichuan region, a three-year-old girl who was trapped for more than 40 hours under the bodies of her parents was pulled to safety, Xinhua said. Rescuers found Song Xinyi yesterday, but were unable to extricate her immediately due to fears the debris above her would collapse. She was fed and shielded from the rain until rescuers extricated her from the rubble.

Premier Wen Jiabao looked over her wounds, part of his highly publicised tour of the disaster area aimed at reassuring the public about the government's response and to show the world that the country is ready to host the Beijing Olympics in August.

Today's leg of the Olympic torch relay in the south-eastern city of Ruijin began with a minute of silence. Wen said 100,000 troops and police had been sent to the disaster zone. East of the epicentre in the town of Hanwang rescuers carried yet more bodies to a makeshift morgue at the Dongqi sports arena. The dead appeared to have come from heavily damaged apartments and a school behind the arena, where people stood in stunned shock.

One of the town's hospitals was obliterated, and another the seven-storey one collapsed, its third floor suddenly smashing to the ground. People on the upper floors climbed out on bed sheets tied together. Surviving medical staff set up a triage centre in the driveway of a tire factory, but could only provide basic care. "The first day hundreds of kids died when a school collapsed. The rest who came in had serious injuries. There was so little we could do for them," said Zhao Xiaoli, a nurse.

"There will be a lot more people. So many still haven't been found," she said.

Residents complained that delays in aid had caused more deaths in the immediate aftermath of the quake. Zhang Chuanlin, a 27-year-old factory worker, said his 52-year-old mother was trapped while watching television with her friend. No rescue workers were around so he started to dig by himself.

"No one was helping me and then two strangers came and dug through the rubble. They found her an hour later," he said. "When they pulled her out I couldn't look, I just couldn't look when they pulled her out." A man who gave only his surname Li said he had suffered a double tragedy. His wife was killed while watching TV with Zhang's mother and his daughter died when her school collapsed. The child did not die right away and could be heard saying, "Please help me daddy, please rescue me," right after the earthquake, he said, but there were no authorities to save her.

As well as informing the reader of the devastation in China, the writer has used a variety of language devices in order to reveal the full extent of the tragedy. The facts alone are disturbing "Official figures put the death toll at nearly 15,000 with 26,000 still buried in rubble and 14,000 missing" though it is the **emotive use of language** which has the greatest impact on the reader.

Look through the highlighted text below which indicates some of the language features used which would have the greatest impact on the reader. Notice that there is also a comment on the impact on the reader.

Extract with highlighted language features	Explanation of the impact on the reader
As help began to arrive in some of the hardest-to-reach areas, some victims trapped for more than two days under collapsed buildings were still being pulled out alive. But the enormous scale of the devastation meant that resources were stretched thin, and makeshift aid stations and refugee centers were springing up over a disaster area the size of Belgium.	The phrase 'hardest to reach' makes the reader feel even more for the victims as we can imagine them being isolated, vulnerable with little help at hand. The words 'trapped' and 'collapsed' evokes a desperate image of the victims being unable to escape. Furthermore, the sheer size of the earthquake is communicated through the words 'enormous' an 'devastation' as well as the description of the disaster area "the size of Belgium". The reader is helped to identify with the sheer helplessness of the situation through the writer's use of personification "resources were stretched thin".

Notice how the quotations used are **relevant, precise and embedded.**

Using the techniques demonstrated in this unit, explain what techniques are used here (highlighted extracts) and what **impact** they have on the reader.

Extract with highlighted language features	Explanation of the impact on the reader
At a middle school Sichuan province's Qingchuan county where students were taking a noon nap when the quake demolished a three-story building, 178 children were confirmed dead in the rubble and another 23 remained missing. Rescuers raced to save people trapped under flattened buildings. East of the epicentre in the town of Hanwang rescuers carried yet more bodies to a makeshift morgue at the Dongqi sports arena. The dead appeared to have come from heavily damaged apartments and a school behind the arena, where people stood in stunned shock. One of the town's hospitals was obliterated, and another the seven-storey one collapsed, its third floor suddenly smashing to the ground.	

Challenge 9 - Create your own success

In this unit you have been looking at how a writer uses language devices. Produce an A5 booklet (half A4) in which you provide advice for other students on how to understand and comment on a writer's use of language. You may wish to use some of the advice below or use your own headings and layout:

- What are language features?
- Why do writers use them?
- Here's some examples of how writers use language
- How do you comment on language?
- Here's some examples of how to comment on writers language.

a) Image response

 **Look at this image and consider all the things that automatically come into your thoughts**

b) Big Question

In a group of two or three, discuss the following question and grade your response as follows:

Who is most responsible for the fact that thousands of people still die from natural disasters?

1) Firstly, you need to consider who could be responsible? (think about the actual disaster and the fact that people die from it)
2) Give an explanation as to why these factors are responsible
3) For each factor give a grade of responsibility (1 most responsible – 5 not responsible)

c) KWL

In pairs, consider the following questions for discussion:
You can only complete the first two columns (K W) at this stage

	K	W	L
What do I already know about:		What do I think I need to know?	What have I learnt?
The British Red Cross			
Cyclones			
Language devices			

In what other subjects could I apply these skills?

In this section you will be looking at web pages from **The British Red Cross**, and in particular considering how they responded to the devastation of a cyclone (a severe storm which creates thunderstorms, winds and flooding rain) which hit Burma.

In order to understand the language devices of any reading text, it is important to establish the purpose first so that any language devices you identify are directly related to what the author (The British Red Cross) are trying to achieve (purpose).

The first part of the web page gives us all the information we need to establish purpose.

 BritishRedCross

What we do

The British Red Cross is a volunteer-led humanitarian organisation that helps people in crisis, whoever and wherever they are.

We enable vulnerable people at home and overseas to prepare for and respond to emergencies in their own communities. And when the crisis is over, we help people recover and move on with their lives.
Help us help people in crisis

Challenge 11

Using this information, briefly summarise what you think is the main purpose of **The British Red Cross**

Now that the purpose of the organisation itself is clearer, you now need to consider how the language used supports the purpose of producing these web pages. The main aims of producing these web pages could be categorised as to

- inform the public of their work;
- promote their cause;
- persuade people to donate;
- recruit more volunteers to support their work;
- reassure the people who have donated (and the many volunteers) that their work is having an impact.

Read through this section **MYANMAR CYCLONE**, and pick out the words and phrases which help to *promote* their cause.

Myanmar cyclone

Why we needed your help
The Red Cross Movement has been at the forefront of the response to the cyclone.

Video: What we are doing
Red Cross teams are helping to build shelters, construct water and sanitation facilities and provide healthcare.

The people we are helping
Read the incredible stories of how Red Cross volunteers have made a life-saving difference to people in Myanmar

Cyclone Nargis photo gallery
View pictures of the devastation caused by Cyclone Nargis and how the Red Cross Movement is responding

Impact of the language used on the reader

In order for The British Red Cross to achieve their aims (outlined earlier) their language choices must have an impact on a wide range of readers. As well as promoting and publicly advertising their cause, they need to actively

- Raise money
- Increase the amount of volunteers

Any organisation which is trying to appeal directly to the public needs to consider the wide range of people who may have access to the information they provide. An audience could be categorised in terms of

- Age – teenagers/adults/pensioners
- Social groupings – working class/middle/upper class/employed/unemployed/students
- Interest groups – people who browse the internet/people who do charity work

How might The British Red Cross appeal to its different audiences?
What type of information and language should be used?

For example, if you are targeting people who are unemployed, it would be unwise to ask for a donation though you could try to persuade them that giving up their free time would be an advantage to themselves as well as the cause.

RECOVERY CONTINUES SIX MONTHS AFTER MYANMAR CYCLONE

31 October 2008

Six months on from Cyclone Nargis, which ripped across the coast of Myanmar on 2 May, more than two million people are endeavouring to rebuild their lives and livelihoods but in many cases, major support is desperately needed.

Liz Hughes, British Red Cross recovery manager, is based in Myanmar and leading the recovery efforts of the International Federation of Red Cross and Red Crescent Societies. She said: "The sheer impact of the devastation is enormous. Our cyclone recovery programmes in Myanmar will continue until April 2011, three years after Nargis made landfall, because of the scale and scope of the rebuilding effort." The cyclone, the worst to hit Asia in over a decade, killed more than 84,000 people and left more than 53,000 missing.

Relief and recovery

In the immediate aftermath of the emergency the British Red Cross raised £1.6 million to support the Myanmar Red Crescent Society which, as a community-based volunteer organisation, was able to begin providing relief immediately. An estimated 1.3 million people in the Ayeyarwady Delta region have received life-saving support through the International Red Cross and Red Crescent Movement. While many of the basic needs have been met, people's livelihoods were severely affected. Over the next two and a half years, the focus for the Red Cross will be on restoring livelihoods and the ability of those affected to generate much-needed income.

The impact on livelihoods can be seen in Kan Thar Yar, a village some 50 kilometres from the Andaman coast, deep inside Labutta township and one of the regions hardest hit by the cyclone. **Livelihoods.**

"Four people lost their lives in this village," said Ba Shwa, a 33-year-old farmer. "More than half the houses were destroyed or damaged, and 21 fishing boats were lost." He added that most of their buffaloes drowned in the floods and the community will now need help to rebuild their homes and their livelihoods.

For the time being, 39 families are crowded together in the few houses that remain standing. To ensure the children have their daily milk, they rent buffaloes from other villages. These rents will, hopefully, be paid for with sacks of rice after the winter harvest in November. The farmers re-planted their devastated paddy fields in July, just in time for the rainy season. However, the seeds they used were not fit for the high saline content in the soil caused by high sea levels during the cyclone, so the outcome of this harvest is uncertain.

Like the majority of people affected by Cyclone Nargis, most families in Kan Thar Yar did not own their own land, but instead cultivated the rice paddies on behalf of landowners. As their livelihood also depends on fishing, they have been doubly penalised with the loss of their boats. "As efforts shift from relief to recovery Red Cross assistance will include psychosocial support programmes to ensure the emotional and practical recovery of those affected, as well as programmes to create income for families whose livelihoods have been destroyed," Liz said.

Using the language of persuasion

The final two pages from the website (Pages 94 and 95) that we are looking at now is the section on why people should volunteer.

It is important to consider the **intended** impact on the **range** of different audiences that The British Red Cross is targeting.

Write a one sentence headline in which you attempt to persuade the following audiences that they should become involved in supporting The British Red Cross (either through donation or volunteering)

- unemployed
- middle/upper class (high earners)
- pensioners
- students

It is important to consider the different ways that the public receive the information (how are people likely to view the web pages/read their leaflets)

Page 92 contains an article regarding the progress of the people of Myanmar six months after the cyclone hit.

As you read through the article on page 92, consider how the public would feel **reassured** that The British Red Cross is having an impact.

How does The British Red Cross use language effectively to persuade young people to volunteer?

Consider:

- use of quotations (people's experience)
- personalised language (directed to the audience)
- informal words and phrases
- how they recognise the needs of young people

Remember when responding to this type of extended question it is important to PEER

Point	The British Red Cross is clearly attempting to persuade its younger audience through its use of personalised language
Evidence	"You're young. You're busy"
Explanation	The language here is direct and personal.
Reader (intended and actual impact on them)	This acknowledgement of a young person's lifestyle will help make volunteering seem more appealing. It would make a young audience feel that their needs are being recognised, therefore making them feel that they should not be inhibited in becoming involved.

Why volunteer with us?

Why volunteer with us?

You're young. You're busy. You've got friends, school, family, work, sports and probably a hundred other commitments. So why spend your precious free time volunteering with the Red Cross?

You'll do great things

Volunteering with the Red Cross is about making a tangible difference to the lives of vulnerable people in your community and around the world. To find out about the incredible ways people of all ages have helped their communities, read about some of our volunteers.

"Volunteering with the Red Cross undoubtedly helped me achieve my goals."

Michelle Yong, intern

It doesn't have to take a lot of time

It's true, some of our voluntary roles require you to take part in training (which we provide). However, we also have opportunities for young people who are short of time. Why not consider using your social networking skills to spread the word about our work by becoming a Red Recruit?

It looks great on your CV

Employers like to see that prospective employees are actively involved in the world around them.

The Red Cross is one of the most respected and best-known humanitarian charities in the world. Showing that you volunteer with us can make your CV stand out in a crowd.

You can learn new things

Whether it's performing first aid, giving presentations or pricing merchandise, most of our voluntary opportunities give you the chance to develop new skills and gain confidence. You can also see from the inside how charities work and whether you might like to make a career in the charity sector.

There are awards to recognise your contribution

Of course you don't volunteer just because you can win an award. But we think it's important to recognise the amazing work our volunteers do, so we promote these awards for young volunteers and encourage you to apply.

True story: From the Red Cross to the BBC

Michelle 24, was an intern with the communications division in London. She said: "I had come from a banking background and was taking a career break to decide what I wanted to do next. I wanted to see what it was like to work for a charity.

"Volunteering with the Red Cross undoubtedly helped me achieve my goals. I grew substantially in confidence and really embraced the friendly and supportive environment."

After interning with the Red Cross, Michelle went on to work for the BBC.

Challenge 16- Future skills

How might I use these skills outside of school?

You are interested in undertaking some voluntary work during your spare time and see the following advertisement from Barnados over the page.

Consider:

- whether this advert would appeal to you
- how the language used in the advert helped you make your decision

Believe in children
Barnardo's

Get involved! - volunteering

We really appreciate all our volunteers, who give us so much by giving some of their time. Getting involved is great fun, flexible, rewarding and sociable, and we can find something for everyone, based on your own interests and skills.

See what some of our volunteers are doing:

The Stars on Saturday Activity Club, which is run as part of Barnardo's Spectrum Project in Hounslow involves over thirty volunteers aged fourteen plus from local schools mixing and making friends with activity club members aged ten to sixteen. All fifteen of the club members have mild to moderate learning difficulties.

Here is what one of our volunteers from Hampton School said:

'I have been a Barnardo's volunteer for seven months now and I am very grateful to have been given this fantastic opportunity to work with a wonderful group of talented children. This experience has made me look at life and other people differently and I am very proud to be a volunteer. Most importantly I have made some great friends.'

But why would you get involved?
Well, there are lots of reasons:-
Get new skills for future jobs and enhance your UCAS form. A recent survey revealed that '3/4 of employers prefer to employ people with volunteering on their CV' (TimeBank and Reed Executive Research, 2001). If requested, we can supply

references to boost your UCAS form or CV.

Gain points for Duke of Edinburgh community reward requirement.
For more information, see **www.theaward.org.**

Develop a wide range of new skills.
These could include presentation and communication, and creative flair and the ability to work in a team or solve problems independently.

Meet new people who think like you
Be independent
Give as much or as little time as you like!

As a volunteer, you could:

- *work in a shop and help as a shop assistant, put your creative flair to use by becoming a window dresser, organise themed glitz and retro events.*

- *help with fundraising by organising your own event or assisting at a Barnardo's event*

- *work directly with children and support small group activities, befriend young people or volunteer at youth clubs and play schemes*

Find out more about what opportunities are available in your area or contact us!

Personalised Progression

Assessment Focus (AF5) Explain and comment on writers' use of language, including grammatical and literary features at word and sentence level

How is my work at KS3 assessed?
Your work is assessed using assessment focuses which help you and your teacher determine on what level your work is currently at. This criteria is often used when assessing your APP work as well as your class work and homework. In this unit we will be looking at how to progress in AF5 (see above)

Key questions:

- What level am I currently working at in this assessment focus for reading? (if unsure, ask your English teacher)
- What skills do I currently have in this assessment focus?
- What skills do I need to develop to get to the next level?

In this section, you will be completing a series of challenges which will show you how you can personally progress to the next level, using many of the skills that you have developed in this unit.

How can I practice my skills to reach the next level in this assessment focus?

- Be clear on what 'language features' actually means
- Ensure that you comment on the intended effects of the language devices and how these impact on the reader
- Provide a personal response to the use of language and comment on to what extend they have been effective

In this assessment focus (AF5), if you are currently working at…

Level 3	go to Progress Checker A (Level 3-4 progression)
Level 4	go to Progress Checker B (Level 4-5 progression)
Level 5	go to Progress Checker C (Level 5-6 progression)
Level 6	go to Progress Checker D (Level 6-7 progression)

When you get to the stage where you feel that you are confident in a particular level in this assessment focus, you can attempt the challenges for the next level.

Progress Checker A – (Level 3-4 reading progression)

Assessment Focus (AF5) – Explain and comment on writers' use of language, including grammatical and literary features at word and sentence level		
I	What level am I currently working at in AF5 reading?	Level 3
	What skills do I currently have in this assessment focus?	As a Level 3 reader in AF5 I am able to: • Identify a few basic features of language though include little or no comment
	What skills do I need to develop to reach the next level?	To be a confident AF5 reader at Level 4 I need to • Identify some basic features of writers' language use • Make a simple comment on the choices that a writer makes

Moving a Level 3 response to Level 4

In order to progress to level 4 in this assessment focus you need to **identify** some basic language features and make a simple comment on the choices made by the writer.

The table below includes a Level 3 response in AF5. Look at how this pupil has achieved this level and think about what they could do to improve.

How does the writer use language to engage the reader in his survival of the Tsunami?	
AF5 – Level 3 response	Why the pupils achieved a Level 3
The writer uses loads of powerful words when telling his story	Basic feature of language is identified (powerful words)

How could we move this response into Level 4?

Although there is a reference to a language feature "powerful words" there needs to be a comment on the writer's choice of words.

AF5 – Level 3 response	AF5 – Level 4 response
The writer uses loads of powerful words like trees snapping when telling his story	*The writer uses loads of powerful words when telling his story "trees snapping" is powerful because it shows he is scared of the waves*

Notice how the Level 4 response provides a comment on the choice of words, rather than just mentioning them.

AF5 Progress Challenge A:

Add a comment to the following sentences which shows that you are beginning to explain a writers' choice of language

When the writer says

The waters were 'surging higher' it is powerful because…

His leg looked like a 'butcher's shop' is disturbing because….

His girlfriend saw people 'clinging in the current, and washed out to sea' is upsetting because….

Progress tip – try using 'because' in your answer after you have identified your point.

Next steps…

Look through your exercise book and highlight how often you make a comment next to a piece of language you have identified. Try to use phrases such as "The writer has used this because".

Progress Checker B – (Level 4-5 reading progression)

Assessment Focus (AF5) – Explain and comment on writers' use of language, including grammatical and literary features at word and sentence level		
1	What level am I currently working at in AF5 reading?	Level 4
2	What skills do I currently have in this assessment focus?	As a Level 4 reader in AF5 I am able to: • Identify some basic features of writers' language use • Make simple comments on writers' choice of language
3	What skills do I need to develop to reach the next level?	To be a confident AF5 reader at Level 5 I need to • Include various features of writers' language with some explanation of these choices • Show some awareness of the effect of writers' language choices

Moving a Level 4 response to Level 5

In order to progress to level 5 in this assessment focus you need to begin **explaining** the choices made and the **effect** on the **reader**.

For example.

AF5 – Level 4 response	**AF5 – Level 5 response**
The writer uses loads of powerful words when telling his story. "trees snapping" is powerful because it shows he is scared of the waves	*The writer uses powerful words such as 'trees snapping' in order for the reader to imagine the power of the waves which makes us feel nervous for him.*

Notice how the Level 5 response provides an **explanation** for the language choice and the way that the **reader** would be **affected**.

AF5 Progress Challenge B

Improve the following sentence by including an explanation as well as a comment on the effect on the reader.

An example has been completed for you.

From ➡	To
After the man kills the girl, the writer makes him speak quickly "Why? Why have I done this?	The writer uses short sentences and rhetorical questions when the man says "Why? Why have I done this?" This makes us read more quickly so that it is like the man feeling tense.
A simile is used in line 3 "she cut through his heart like a knife through butter" which shows she is mean to him.	

Next steps…

Look through your exercise book and highlight every time you have picked out a language feature (i.e adjective/simile/sentence structure etc) In a different coloured pen, include an explanation as well as a comment on effect on the reader.

Progress Checker C – (Level 5-6 reading progression)

Assessment Focus (AF5) – Explain and comment on writers' use of language, including grammatical and literary features at word and sentence level		
I	What level am I currently working at in AF5 reading?	Level 5
	What skills do I currently have in this assessment focus?	As a Level 5 reader in AF5 I am able to: • include various features of writers' language with some explanation of these choices • show some awareness of the effect of writers' language choices
	What skills do I need to develop to reach the next level?	To be a confident AF5 reader at Level 6 I need to • provide a detailed explanation of the language choices • use appropriate terminology of how language is used • draw together how a range of language choices has on the overall effect on the reader

Moving a Level 5 response to Level 6

In order to progress to level 6 in this assessment focus you need to use **detailed** explanations as well as being clear on the language **terminology**. It is also important to consider how the **range** of language used by a writer has on the **overall effect** on the reader.

For example.

AF5 – Level 5 response	Why the pupils achieved a Level 5
The writer uses powerful words such as 'trees snapping' in order for the reader to imagine the power of the waves which makes us feel nervous for him.	*Language feature identified* *Explanation* *Effect of the writer's choices*

How could we move this response into Level 6?

- More detailed explanation
- Use terminology more (not just powerful words)
- Consider the range of language features and how they contribute to the overall effect on the reader

AF5 – Level 5 response	AF5 – Level 6 response
The writer uses powerful words such as 'trees snapping' in order for the reader to imagine the power of the waves which makes us feel nervous for him.	*The writer uses his senses to describe the devastation of his situation "I feel I could scarcely hear in that thunder" which makes the reader feel that he must have been in some kind of trance. This creates a feeling of anticipation, particularly when be begins to describe the sound of the 'trees snapping'*

Notice how the Level 6 response comments on the specific terminology 'senses' as well as giving a range of language features which contributes to the overall effect on the reader.

AF5 Progress Challenge C

A student has produced a good level 5 response to the question below, using the extract provided.

What advice would you include for this student to achieve a Level 6?

How does the writer use language effectively in this passage to help the reader identify with his desperate situation?

We limped up to the road, and then we could hear the screaming and wailing of people that had just made it, they had just lost loved ones, we're just starting to realise what had happened, and now we're watching as other waves were approaching. Small clumps of people by the road now started to panic and run up into the hills. We followed, barefoot, in our underwear, feeling like aboriginal natives running into the jungle. I could hardly put weight on my leg, and the blood was coming down in small spurts as my flesh split from my tourniquets with the movement.

Level 5 response:
The words 'screaming' and wailing' make us feel sorry for him as he must have been frightened. He says they were like 'aboriginal natives' which makes them sound desperate.

Progress Checker D – (Level 6-7 reading progression)

Assessment Focus (AF5) – Explain and comment on writers' use of language, including grammatical and literary features at word and sentence level		
I	What level am I currently working at in AF5 reading?	Level 6
	What skills do I currently have in this assessment focus?	As a Level 6 reader in AF5 I am able to: • provide a detailed explanation of the language choices • use appropriate terminology of how language is used • draw together how a range of language choices has on the overall effect on the reader
	What skills do I need to develop to reach the next level?	To be a confident Level 7 reader at AF5 I need to • develop precise, perceptive analysis of how language is used • show appreciation of how the writer's language choices contribute to the overall meaning

Moving a Level 6 response to Level 7

In order to progress to level 7 in this assessment focus you need to appreciate the reasons why language choices are made by a writer as well as considering how the range of language features used contribute to the overall effect on the reader. Look at the differences between the responses over the page to the question:

How does the writer engage the reader in his survival?

Even almost three weeks after the accident, my relatively small wounds are still seeping with fluid discharge, but the swelling has gone down, and we hope the infections are under control.

We still can hardly believe how lucky we were. If we had been in any less sturdy of a bungalow, we could easily have been crushed, as we saw many other concrete structures crushed. If we had spent a few more minutes at brunch, or woke up a little later, we could have been on the beach when the waters came, and have been crushed again and separated by miles when the waters picked up everything in their path. If the waters had come up 8 inches higher, we would have drowned in our bungalows. If my thigh wound had been another inch or two over, my artery would have been cut, or if we couldn't get to the first hospital, I could have easily bled to death. And if we didn't get to Bangkok as quickly as we did, my wounds could have become infected leading to amputation or worse. But all that didn't happen to us.

Level 6 response	Level 7 response
The reader shares in the man's survival and can feel his relief at only having 'relatively minor wounds'. He uses the graphic verb of 'seeping' to help us visualise his suffering, yet he acknowledges that they were lucky, highlighted by the short sentence "But all that didn't happen to us"	*Clearly, the reader is expected to feel sympathy for the man; his 'seeping' wounds and the 'fluid discharge' evoke images of pain and suffering as does his description of his current state "we hope the infections are under control" The use of the word 'hope' creates a feeling of uncertainty for the reader, and helps us share in his continual journey of survival. The writer further engages us with his survival through the powerful use of verb "crushed" and "bled" (to death) which describes what could have happened; his final short sentence "But all that didn't happen to us" has clearly been created to evoke a feeling of closure for himself and his reader*

Notice here how the Level 7 response explains **how and why** language devices have been used; it also shows **appreciation** of how the language devices combined creates the overall effect.

What is needed to make the next step?

One of the most effective techniques to use when helping to progress to level 7+ in AF5 reading is to ensure that you view each piece of text as a result of a carefully constructed piece of work that includes many tools (language devices) that have been consciously used by the writer to achieve a particular effect on the reader. Once you have began to consider the reasons for the language choices and begin hypothising as to how they affect the reader in different ways, you are getting into Level 7 territory.

AF5 Progress Challenge D

Use the advice from this chapter to make a dictionary of language devices. For example, use of similes, adjectives, emotive language etc. For each one, attempt to write an example of how this could be used effectively for a range of effects. The example below is from Macbeth

Language device	Example	Appreciation of how the language choice creates a particular effect
Personification	"Out, out brief candle. Life is but a walking shadow"	to create sympathy for Lady Macbeth to show the moral difference between Macbeth and Lady Macbeth. to reveal the more human side of Macbeth's character to reveal Shakespeare's reflections on the temporary nature of life.

When could I use these skills outside of school?

Programme of Study Links	**Competence** Reading and understanding a range of texts, and responding appropriately. **Critical understanding** Assessing the validity and significance of information and ideas from different sources.
Framework Objectives	Understanding and responding to ideas, viewpoints, themes and purposes in texts.
Personal Learning & Thinking Skills	**Enquiry** predicting outcomes. **Evaluation** judging the value of what is read. **Reasoning** using precise language to explain thought processes.
AFL	Peer assessment. Writing own success criteria.
Assessment Focus	**AF6:** - identify and comment on writers' purposes and viewpoints, and the overall effect of the text on the reader.
Functional Skills	**Preparation for employment** research and presentation skills.

Challenge 1- Get thinking

In pairs, consider the following points for discussion

a) What might the following line tell us about someone's attitude towards tackling yob culture (youth crime)

"If it were up to me I'd use a sledgehammer to crack a nut."

b) Provide an example of how this approach might be done in practice.

c) Think of a different metaphor to describe someone having a different approach.

For example:

If it were down to me I'd use an oven glove to take the heat out of the situation

d) Read through the following words and place them in the appropriate category. The learning from this challenge is about the discussion that takes place – there is not one definitive answer though you will need to explain why you have made these decisions.

In what other subjects could I apply these skills?

achieve   alienating   broken   condemn   criticise   demand   dismay
employ   heal   hoodies   initiative   invested   offered   rotten
stabbed   success   tackle   understand   urge

Descriptions of society (people and places)	Actions taken (verbs used)	Plans for the future

Chapter 5

Below is an overview of how you will develop your skills as an effective and critical reader in this unit.

In this unit I will learn how to effectively... *(Learning Objectives)*	• respond to a writer's ideas, viewpoints and purposes • make a personal response to a text, using evidence effectively
The topics I will be studying are... *(Stimulus)*	**Yob Culture** *The Sun's* article on 'Broken Britain' *UK Youth Parliament* Discussion Forum *The Sun's* Enough is Enough article
My understand will be checked by seeing how I... *(Assessment Criteria)*	Identify and comment on writers' purposes and viewpoints, and the overall effect of the text on the reader (AF6)
My achievement will be demonstrated through me successfully completing the following challenges: *(Learning Outcomes)*	Challenge 1 'Get thinking' discussion activity Challenge 2 Article analysis Challenge 3 Development of argument Challenge 4 Organising main arguments Challenge 5 Creating your own success Challenge 6 'Get thinking' – drama role play Challenge 7 Making notes effectively Challenge 8 Extended answer Challenge 9 Supporting each other's success. Challenge 10 'Get thinking'. Image analysis Challenge 11 Diagram activity Challenge 12 Article analysis Challenge 13 Future skills Progress Challenges

For the following challenges, you will be asked to specifically consider how Sir Alan Sugar presents his arguments to the reader. As mentioned in previous chapters, you must always **read for a purpose** and in this case, you need to consider the following two aspects:

1. What is Sir Alan Sugar's purpose?
2. What techniques does he use to try and achieve this?

Once these have been examined at length, you will then need to **make a personal response** to the article in which you consider whether it is successful in achieving its purpose.

SIR ALAN SUGAR'S DISMAY AT 'BROKEN' BRITAIN

By Sam Wilson

Sir Alan Sugar has criticised the state of modern Britain and called for billions of pounds to be invested in the police force to tackle yob culture.

Speaking exclusively to The Sun newspaper, the Amstrad tycoon, 61, demanded "radical" investment from the Government to put thousands more police on the streets.

The Apprentice guru, thought to be worth £880 million, also urged youngsters to use their initiative to achieve success in business, craft, or sport rather than relying on state handouts.

Sir Alan went on to condemn the "crazy" human rights laws he claims are preventing police and teachers from doing their jobs, and criticised the parents of hoodies for alienating their teenagers by ignoring them. He said: "It has gone bloody mad out there. It really is 'Broken Britain'. Something needs to be done and it has got to be radical. No half measures.

"It's beyond my comprehension that I hear every day of someone being stabbed. It's like the weather. You know it's going to happen, you just read to find out the details."

Sir Alan, who began working at the age of 16 and went on to become one of Britain's most successful entrepreneurs, called for the Government to take bold action to heal Britain's "broken" society.

He said: *"If it were up to me I'd use a sledgehammer to crack a nut.*

Sir Alan Sugar is a big hit in TV's The Apprentice

The Government needs to invest more money in the police force.

"And I'm not talking about a couple of extra Bobbies on the beat in each borough. I'm talking about real investment.

"This Government has shown it can put huge sums of money behind causes it believes in. Look at the Iraq war - billions were spent on that and we're still spending now."

"Imagine if the kind of money we threw at that situation went into more police. The rotten kids out there need to be the ones who are worried — worried they're going to be in a world of trouble if they cause offence."

Sir Alan, who grew up on a tough council estate in East London, offered troublemakers an olive branch by urging ministers to invest in community projects and youth centres "where kids can go and feel good about themselves."

He said: *"We need to work with hoodies to understand them better, to find out why they've chosen the route they have. It's a flaw in the education system so maybe it's hard for this to happen at schools.*

"We need to employ people to give them somewhere to go. Eventually some might get off their backsides and get a job."

"If it were up to me I'd use a sledgehammer to crack a nut. The Government needs to invest more money in the police force."

Sir Alan Sugar

On your own, record your initial thoughts on this article, using the prompts below as a guide:

- What are the main points Sir Alan Sugar is making?
- How successful do you think he is making them on a scale 1-5 (1 not successful – 5 totally convinced by his ideas)

Explain your decisions to your work partner

Challenge 3

Which of the following statements best describes the way that Sir Alan Sugar develops his argument?

1. He considers alternative viewpoints before giving his own.
2. He is critical of the government and parents and thinks we should do more.
3. He shows understanding of the pressures that the government and parents are under.

How is the argument developed so convincingly?

In this article, one of the main reason why Sir Alan is able to **communicate** his thoughts on youth crime so successfully is through the **techniques** he uses to have an **impact** on the **audience**.

For example, he uses

- **Powerful words and phrases** to attract the audience's attention "Broken Britain", "get off their backsides"
- **Repetition** (notice how many references he makes to money and extra finance)
- **Assertive language** which helps to voice his personal opinions "If it were up to me", "We need to work", "Something needs to be done"
- **Supports the arguments** made (he uses the example of how much was spent on the unpopular war in Iraq)

What strategies could I use to progress further?

What has helped me learn effectively today?

The following table has examples of the main arguments used in the article. They have been categorised in the top row though you may wish to choose your own heading. Find 2-3 examples from the article for each column which helps/supports the points made. A couple have been completed for you.

Views on society *(in general)*	Criticism *(of the government, schools and parents)*	Solutions *Advice to youngsters and how to overcome the problem*
- Dismay at 'Broken Britain' - Criticised the state of modern Britain - It's beyond my comprehension that I hear every day of someone being stabbed	- Condemn the "crazy" human rights laws - Criticised the parents of hoodies for alienating their teenagers by ignoring them	- Youngsters to use their initiative to achieve success - Billions of pounds to be invested - "Radical" investment - Something needs to be done

Challenge 5 - Creating your own success

When could I use these skills outside of school?

Who wants to be a fiver richer?
In your pairs, you need to produce a series of questions (5) which you believe would most effectively help other students to understand how Sir Alan Sugar develops his argument.

In the style of Who wants to be a Millionaire, the questions need to get progressively harder – you must also provide 3 wrong answers, though don't make it too obvious which 3 are wrong!

You may wish to use some of the sentence starters below:

- Explain how the writer presents…
- Suggest a reason why…
- His main argument was…
- The writer is convincing because…
- Sir Alan supports this point by…

In threes, organise yourselves into the following roles:

- Young offender (just been arrested for stealing a car and joy-riding)
- Police officer (who has just arrested the youth)
- Parent of young offender

Before you begin a discussion, each person needs to prepare some ideas on the following questions:

1) What are the reasons for the crime?
2) What are the solutions?

You now need to discuss this issue from the point of view of the character you have been given.

Between the three of you, choose the three most effective solutions you have come up with to tackle the problem of young people offending.

The web pages that you will find over the page are from the *UK Youth Parliament*, which is an organisation run by young people for young people; its aims are to give a voice to young people aged between 11 - 18 and to impact on organisations that provide services for young people. These web pages show an overview of the organisation, followed by extracts from an on-line discussion that took place on the topic of: **A change of how young people are seen.**

Challenge 7

As you read through these pages, consider what are **the main arguments** put forward by each teenager. Their online names are below. Copy out the table and record their arguments as you read the text. This means you will need to **read actively** as shown in chapter 1. As well as recording their arguments, you also need to record how much you value their opinion, as well as making your own response to their ideas. You may wish to ask a question or give your own alternative idea. (Use chapter 2 for advice on making notes effectively)

	Summary of their main points	**Any good? 1-5** **1= fantastic idea** **5= Not worth considering**	**My response to the points they make**
make.me.smile			
Hamsterwaffle			
Matt. P			
Vampiress			

In what other subjects could I apply these skills?

What strategies could I use to progress further?

http://www.ukyouthparliament.org.uk
Welcome to the UK Youth Parliament website

About UK Youth ParliamentLast

The UK Youth Parliament (UKYP) enables young people to use their energy and passion to change the world for the better. Run by young people for young people, UKYP gives the young people of the UK, between the age of 11 and 18 a voice, which is heard and listened to by local and national government, providers of services for young people and other agencies who have an interest in the views and needs of young people.

make.me.smile

Mainly, we are seen as a bunch of incapable antisocial yobs, who are planning on living on benefits for the rest of our lives. Even though most people do know this, they still don't particularly "trust" young people. Politicians in general, I feel, do not know how to get through to us, which I have to say I can understand seeing how little people are involved in these forums for example. What do you think we can do to get more young people involved in politics? Because more people means more power, and at the moment I don't see us making enough of a difference.

Hamsterwaffle

I think a good way of improving young people's image in the community would be for us to take an active role in fighting anti-social behaviour. A way of doing this would be for the police to be given funding to employ young people to assist in policing anti social areas. They would work for less money and would help combat the sense that there is no police presence on the streets.

Matt. P

I understand the message given out here, but many of these yobs don't even respect the police, what can a couple of youths without any of the police's power and authority do? And if we gave full power to these young people, there is always the chance of people misusing it. There's nothing a bully likes more than organised violence with the support of the state behind them-it has been done many times before.

Hamsterwaffle

At all times there would be, for example, 5 of the youth police to 1 policeman in one small area.

Vampiress

I don't think youth violence and such is that big of a problem. I mean, it's a problem of course but I think the government uses the stuff that a couple of us do and broadcast it to draw attention away from other issues. We do need to change our image but good luck trying to teach the British Electoral System to a class full of students with the attention span of 5cm.

make.me.smile

Again, no need to start insulting people, many people just don't feel it's worth getting involved as it is so hard to get heard. Anyway, no one has come up with any ideas. So how about: -As hamster suggested, some kind of system meaning no more ASBOs and instead the young offenders have to do some kind of community work, though I don't think letting them patrol the streets would work. I was thinking more cleaning, repairing and whatever. -More advertising for organisations like UKYP -More involvement of young people in parliament; -Compulsory politics/citizenship classes in all schools; in all this though, as always, we need schools' government's and parents' help - how do we get this idea across?

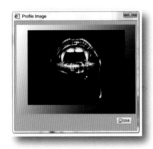

Vampiress
You must have misinterpreted my post as for once I wasn't trying to be insulting although I have been told I'm sometimes too direct so I apologise for not cushioning up my post. I was just highlighting the point that while we want to change our image the wider variety of teens may not be so willing to do the work needed.

make.me.smile
Don't cushion your posts. Anyway it is true that it is young people's fault, but also the media's. And even if most teens can't be bothered to change their image, doesn't mean we should let it happen, as it affects all of us.

Vampiress
You say that now! It does, but what would be the point if, while we worked to repair the damage, others caused more? It would just be a never ending circle.

Matt.P
"You cut your fingernails, even though you know they'll grow back"

Just because something will be hard and long-lasting, doesn't mean it's not worth doing and is not a reason for putting it off indefinitely.

Collecting your ideas for an extended answer

In the first two challenges you looked at the topics of

- Why young people may offend
- How they can be viewed better by the outside world

Using the ideas that you have discussed and recorded, complete the challenge in the box below. To help with this challenge, the key words have been recorded with explanations of how best to respond to this answer.

> **Analyse and respond to the main arguments put forward on the UK Youth Parliament website on how changes could be put in place on how young people are seen by society.**
>
> **Analyse (Consider in detail/ work out the meaning)**
>
> **Respond (Give a personal opinion to the arguments made)**
>
> **Main arguments (The key points made by each person in the discussion)**

You will need to show that you can

- Identify the main purpose and ideas
- Make a personal response

Challenge 9 - supporting each other's success

In pairs you need to look at each other's work in order to make improvements. To be able to do this well, you need to know the criteria for what a good response looks like.

Use the table below and record your thoughts on your work partner's response to Challenge 3. Remember to give advice on how to improve.

	Scale 1-5 1= fantastic idea 5= Not worth considering	Example of this	How it could be improved – what could have been included to get a better response?
Identify the main purpose and ideas			
Make a personal response			

In what other subjects could I apply these skills?

a) With your work partner, look carefully through the image below and discuss the following:

1) What is happening?
2) What may have previously happened?
3) Who is involved?
4) How are the people feeling in the picture?
5) What clues in the picture have helped with this discussion?

From your discussion, choose a newspaper headline which you feel best sums up what the picture (and story behind the picture) is about.

a) Read through the following list of questions.

Mums and dads, when did you last really check where your son or daughter was going at night?
Who are they hanging around with?
What do they get up to when your backs are turned?

1) Where do you think this is from?
2) Who has said it?
3) Who is it for?
4) Why has it been written?

As you read through the article on the next two pages, consider:

- What message is the newspaper trying to get across? (purpose)
- How does it get across its message? (style/layout)
- Who is it aiming at and what reaction is it hoping for? (audience)
- How do you respond to the article? (personal response)

It's time to say ... NO MORE

FATAL knifing of Robert Knox takes number of teens violently killed in London this year to 14

We'll miss you so much ... grim-faced friends look over floral tributes and T-shirts at the spot where Rob was killed.

Killed ... Rob

That was the heart-felt plea yesterday by murdered teenager Rob Knox's tearful Gran Margaret. And she spoke for the whole of Britain, including The Sun, when she begged parents to teach their kids respect for life. Only then will the tide of teenage savagery, which has claimed the young victims on this page and crushed their families, be turned.

The nation is in the grip of an epidemic of deadly youth violence. Teenagers are having lives that are full of potential snuffed out by mindless stabbings, shootings and mob beatings. The toll is mounting almost daily. The names of the victims are becoming all too familiar — including Rhys Jones, Jimmy Mizen, Adam Regis, Etem Celebi, Evren Anil, David Nowak. On Saturday, 18-year-old Rob Knox. And on Sunday the latest to fall, 17- year-old Amar Aslam. Yet little is done to stop the bloodshed.

- **By politicians** who pay lip service to preventing street crimc.

- **By Judges** and magistrates who treat feral thugs with kid gloves.

- **And by mothers and fathers** who simply don't try hard enough to be PARENTS — and inevitably blame someone else when it all goes tragically wrong.

Rob's grieving Gran hits the nail on the head when she says: "Any idiot can have a baby but bringing them up well is tough."

Challenge

"There are babies being born today to people who are children themselves."
"These parents challenge the teachers, challenge the police. It's always someone else's responsibility." "All of us have a part to play — for we are in this nightmare together."

Mums and dads, when did you last really check where your son or daughter was going at night? Who are they hanging around with?
What do they get up to when your backs are turned?

The Government must respond, too. And quickly, for there is not a moment to lose. Five months ago Prime Minister Gordon Brown promised The Sun a crackdown on knife crime in a dozen "hotspots" around Britain. Today he must extend it nationwide.

The Sun also demands automatic PROSECUTION for those caught with a knife, and an immediate end to them getting away with just a police caution. Thousands of KNIFE DETECTORS should be given to police. And they should waste no time in using them. JUDGES should hand down jail terms for anyone convicted of violent intent with a knife.

Justice Secretary Jack Straw must provide more PRISON PLACES. And he should deliver the prison ship he has repeatedly promised Sun readers. Mr Brown is desperate to prove he is listening to the nation. Now, it is time for him to act.

Before yet another young life is taken by a blade of cold steel.

a) In pairs, produce a diagram below which you can use to record your thoughts on the article. At this stage, write a brief comment in each section.

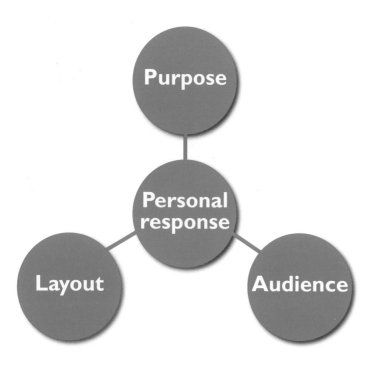

- **What message is the newspaper trying to get across?** (purpose)
- **How does it get across its message?** (style/layout)
- **Who is it aiming at and what reaction is it hoping for?** (audience)
- **How do you respond to the article?**

b) The next question to consider is **how** the article achieves its aims. In particular, what techniques does it use to impact on its audience.

From your discussion during **challenge 6** you may have considered that the article is **informative** and **persuasive** in its tone. You will notice that the story is not covering a new event – Rob Knox had been killed previously – though *The Sun* is using the powerful images and the disturbing facts of that particular case, to support their **commentary** on youth knife crime.

Challenge 12

How does the article communicate effectively to its audience on the issue of youth knife crime?

You may use some of the prompts below to support your answer:

- layout
- language used
- effect on the reader
- your own personal response

Use of pictures and captions

We'll miss you so much... grim-faced friends
look over floral tributes and
T-shirts at the spot where Rob was killed
**Use of 'We'll' helps the reader identify
with the suffering**

Killed ... Rob
Short, powerful caption

Heartache… family comfort each other
Use of emotive noun – 'heartache'

Use of language

In pairs, discuss why the words and phrases may have been highlighted.
Think about whether they may be

- adjectives/verbs/adverbs
- imperatives(commanding statement)
- rhetorical questions
- emotive language/simile/metaphor/personification/alliteration

Some words and phrases use more than one language device.
i.e. begged is a verb and it is also emotive.

FATAL (adjective) knifing of Robert Knox takes number of teens **violently** killed in London this year to 14

That was the **heart-felt** plea yesterday by murdered teenager Rob Knox's **tearful** Gran Margaret. And she spoke for the whole of Britain, including The Sun, when she **begged** parents to teach their kids respect for life. Only then will **the tide of teenage savagery**, (personification) which has claimed the young victims on this page and **crushed** their families, be turned.

The nation is in the **grip** of an **epidemic** of **deadly** youth violence.

Teenagers are having lives that are full of potential **snuffed out** by mindless stabbings, shootings and mob beatings. The toll is mounting almost daily. The names of the victims are becoming all too familiar — including Rhys Jones, Jimmy Mizen, Adam Regis, Etem Celebi, Evren Anil, David Nowak. On Saturday, 18-year-old Rob Knox. And on Sunday the latest to fall, 17- year-old Amar Aslam.

Yet little is done to stop the **bloodshed**.

- By politicians who pay lip service to preventing street crime.

- By judges and magistrates who treat **feral thugs** with kid gloves.

- And by mothers and fathers who **simply don't try hard enough** to be PARENTS — and inevitably blame someone else when it all goes tragically wrong.

Rob's **grieving Gran** (adjective/alliteration) hits the nail on the head when she says:

"Any idiot can have a baby but bringing them up well is tough."
Challenge
"There are babies being born today to people who are children themselves."
"These parents challenge the teachers, challenge the police." "It's always someone else's responsibility." "All of us have a part to play — for we are in this **nightmare** together."
Mums and dads, **when did you last really check where your son or daughter was going at night?**
Who are they hanging around with?
What do they get up to when your backs are turned? Rhetorical questions

The Government must respond, too. And quickly, for there is not a moment to lose. Five months ago Prime Minister Gordon Brown promised The Sun a crackdown on knife crime in a dozen "hotspots" around Britain. Today he must extend it nationwide. **The Sun also demands** (imperatives) automatic **PROSECUTION** for those caught with a knife, and an **immediate** end to them getting away with just a police caution.

Thousands of KNIFE DETECTORS should be given to police. And they should waste no time in using them. JUDGES should hand down jail terms for anyone convicted of violent intent with a knife.

Justice Secretary Jack Straw **must provide** more PRISON PLACES. And **he should deliver** the prison ship he has repeatedly promised Sun readers. Mr Brown is desperate to prove he is listening to the nation. **Now, it is time** for him to act.

Effect on the reader

It is important that you put yourself in the point of view of the **intended** reader, even if you are not personally affected by the article; it is important also to identify with the audience who may be affected personally by such events. How would your parents/carers respond differently to you?

Personal response This is where you have the opportunity to give your own personal viewpoint, although it must be directly related to the question set; therefore, you will need to comment on how successful (or otherwise) the article is in communicating its purpose to its audience. What impact did it have on you – were the devices that were used effective and why?
What could have had more impact?

Challenge 13 - Future skills

How might I use these skills outside of school?

You have decided to apply for a part time post as a Youth Community Worker and have been asked to do a presentation on the following topic:

1) What are the challenges that young people face today?
2) How would you try and promote a more positive image of young people?

In your presentation, you may wish to use some of the information from this chapter, particularly:

- Sir Alan Sugar's comments on what should be done on youth crime (Broken Britain)
- The views of teenagers that were expressed by the UK Youth Parliament
- The comments by *The Sun* and the people involved in the Rob Knox story

What is needed in an effective presentation?

Ability to:

- **speak clearly and confidently**
- **keep eye contact with your audience**
- **use gestures where appropriate**
- **vary tone and pace**
- **use other resources effectively to support your ideas**
- **answer questions effectively**

Personalised Progression

Assessment Focus (AF6) Identify and comment on writers' purposes and viewpoints, and the overall effect of the text on the reader.

How is my work at KS3 assessed?

Your work is assessed using assessment focuses which help you and your teacher determine on what level your work is currently at. This criteria is often used when assessing your APP work as well as your class work and homework. In this unit we will be looking at how to progress in AF6 (see above)

Key questions:

- What level am I currently working at in this assessment focus for reading? (if unsure, ask your English teacher)
- What skills do I currently have in this assessment focus?
- What skills do I need to develop to get to the next level?

In this section, you will be completing a series of challenges which will show you how you can personally progress to the next level, using many of the skills that you have developed in this unit.

How can I practice my skills to reach the next level in this assessment focus?

- Remember that the texts that you are asked to read are not necessarily aimed at you
- Consider the different audiences that a writer may be aiming at.
  For example:
  Age/class/occupation/interest group/gender
- Empathise with the needs of the target audience before commenting on whether the writer achieves his/her purpose.
- When reading a text, look for visual clues that inform you of the writers' viewpoint and purpose. For example, a logo from a company often indicates that the purpose is for you to buy something from them.
- At home, find a variety of reading materials – magazines, newspapers, adverts (particularly the free ads that come through your letterbox) Think about who each one is aiming at and whether it is effective.
- Once you have worked out who it is aimed at, try to find the target audience at home and ask them whether it is effective. For example, you could ask an elderly relative whether they think an advert for a chair lift is convincing – or ask your cat whether the latest cat food advert is appealing (only joking – though you get the idea!)

In this assessment focus (AF6), if you are currently working at...

Level 3	**go to Progress Checker A (Level 3-4 progression)**
Level 4	**go to Progress Checker B (Level 4-5 progression)**
Level 5	go to Progress Checker C (Level 5-6 progression)
Level 6	**go to Progress Checker D (Level 6-7 progression)**

When you get to the stage where you feel that you are confident in a particular level in this assessment focus, you can attempt the challenges for the next level.

Progress Checker A – (Level 3-4 reading progression)

Assessment Focus (AF6) – Identify and comment on writers' purposes and viewpoints, and the overall effect of the text on the reader.		
I	What level am I currently working at in AF6 reading?	Level 3
	What skills do I currently have in this assessment focus?	As a Level 3 reader in AF6 I am able to: • make comments which show I understand the main purpose of the text • give a personal opinion though I am not aware of the writers' viewpoint or effect on the reader
	What skills do I need to develop to reach the next level?	To be a confident AF6 reader at Level 4 I need to • identify the main purpose of the text • show some awareness of the writers' viewpoint • make a simple comment on the overall effect on the reader

Moving a Level 3 response to Level 4

In order to progress to level 4 in this assessment focus you need to **identify** the main **purpose** and show awareness of the **viewpoint** and **effect** on the reader.

The table below includes a Level 3 response in AF6. Look at how this pupil has achieved this level and think about what they could do to improve.

What does Sir Alan Sugar want to get across to his audience in his article on youth crime?	
AF6 – Level 3 response	Why the pupils achieved a Level 3
Alan Sugar wants young people to stop being violent which I agree with.	*Main purpose is identified and there is a personal response made.*

How could we move this response into Level 4?

Although there is a **simple comment** on the message that Sir Alan wants to get across to his audience, it is undeveloped, with **little awareness** of the writer's **viewpoint** or the **effect** on the reader.

What is needed to make the next step?

One of the most effective techniques to use when helping to progress to level 4 + is to be clearer on the purpose and show awareness of the writer's viewpoint and effect on the reader.

For example.

AF6 – Level 3 response	**AF6 – Level 4 response**
Alan Sugar wants young people to stop being violent which I agree with.	*Alan Sugar wants young people to stop being violent and wants something done about it. He makes you think that people should do more to help them.*

Notice how the Level 4 response is clearer on the purpose of the article. Sir Alan Sugar is not just commenting on youth crime, he specifically wants action to be taken. The level 4 response included this and therefore showed awareness of the writer's viewpoint. Rather than simply saying "I agree with" which is a Level 3 type of understanding, the level 4 response begins to identify with the effect on the reader.

AF6 Progress Challenge A:

Change the following sentences by showing awareness of the writer's viewpoint

> *(extract from The Sun newspaper on youth crime)*
> Mums and dads, when did you last really check where your son or daughter was going at night?
> Who are they hanging around with?
> What do they get up to when your backs are turned?

In these lines it is checking to see where the children are and I make sure that I am home if my mum is worried about me.

Progress tip – try using a connective to explain your answer.

Next steps…Look through your exercise book and highlight how often you comment on the writer's purpose. You could also make sure that you use connecting statement in order to help explain your answers more fully. For example: because…/so…/he says this so that../ we think this because…/ I know this…

Progress Checker B – (Level 4-5 reading progression)

AF6 – Identify and comment on writers' purposes and viewpoints, and the overall effect of the text on the reader.		
I	What level am I currently working at in AF6 reading?	Level 4
	What skills do I currently have in this assessment focus?	As a Level 4 reader in AF6 I am able to: • make comments which show I understand the main purpose of the text • give a personal opinion though I am not aware of the writers' viewpoint or effect on the reader
	What skills do I need to develop to reach the next level?	To be a confident AF6 reader at Level 5 I need to • identify the main purpose of the text • show some awareness of the writers' viewpoint • make a simple comment on the overall effect on the reader

Moving a Level 4 response to Level 5

In order to progress to level 5 in this assessment focus you need to **clearly identify** the main **purpose** and provide an **explanation** of the **viewpoint** and **effect** on the reader.

Read through the task and the example below. Look at how this pupil has achieved this level and think about what they could do to improve.

How does Matt P respond to the idea that young people should be used by the police with helping remove youth violence?

Matt P
I understand the message given out here, but many of these yobs don't even respect the police, what can a couple of youths without any of the police's power and authority do? And if we gave full power to these young people, there is always the chance of people misusing it. There's nothing a bully likes more than organised violence with the support of the state behind them - its been done many times before.

AF6 – Level 4 response	Why the pupils achieved a Level 4
Matt P believes that young people won't work well with the police which might make teenagers angry.	*Main purpose is identified and a simple comment is made on the effect on the reader*

How could we move this response into Level 5?
The purpose of the writer's views needs more explanation as it is a little limited. There also needs to be a clearer understanding of how the audience might respond to this point of view.

What is needed to make the next step?
One of the most effective techniques to use when helping to progress to level 5+ in AF6 reading is to ensure that each statement you make regarding the writer's purpose and viewpoint includes a reference to the text that is explained; also, it is important to explain your views on the effect on the reader.

For example.

AF6 – Level 4 response	AF6 – Level 5 response
Matt P believes that young people won't work well with the police which might make teenagers angry.	*Matt P believes that young people won't work well with the police because he says they "don't even respect the police". Some teenagers might be angry at this comment because they feel they could be trusted.*

Notice how the Level 5 response provides a quotation and explanation (in red) which helps to explain the answer more clearly for the reader.

AF6 Progress Challenge B

Read through the extract below and the responses that are given to the task set. What advice (and alternative answers) would you give to the students who came up with these responses?

How effective is the UK Youth Parliament in communicating its message to its audience?

> **About UK Youth Parliament**
> The UK Youth Parliament (UKYP) enables young people to use their energy and passion to change the world for the better. Run by young people for young people, UKYP gives the young people of the UK, between the age of 11 and 18 a voice, which is heard and listened to by local and national government, providers of services for young people and other agencies who have an interest in the views and needs of young people.

- *It is working for kids*
- *It gives you a voice*
- *It has loads of people listening to them*
- *It's about kids talking about other kids*

Next steps…

When reading a text in class or at home, put yourself in the position of the target audience and ask questions back to the text. Swap with a work partner and see if they can answer it for you; this may help you identify more clearly with the needs of the target audience and whether it achieves its aims.

Progress Checker C – (Level 5-6 reading progression)

AF6 – Identify and comment on writers' purposes and viewpoints, and the overall effect of the text on the reader.		
I	What level am I currently working at in AF6 reading?	Level 5
	What skills do I currently have in this assessment focus?	As a Level 5 reader in AF6 I am able to: • clearly identify the main purpose through a general overview • clearly identify the viewpoint, with some, often limited, explanation. • show awareness of the effect on the reader with some, often limited, explanation.
	What skills do I need to develop to reach the next level?	To be a confident AF6 reader at Level 6 I need to • identify the main purpose of the text through using evidence precisely. • clearly identify and explain a writers' viewpoint through close reference to the text • explicitly explain how effects have been created on the reader

Moving a Level 5 response to Level 6

In order to progress to level 6 in this assessment focus you need to use evidence **precisely** as well as **explaining** the writers' viewpoint through **closely referring** to the text. It is not enough just to comment on the effect on the reader (a level 5 skill), you also need to comment on **how this effect** has been created.
For example:

AF6 – Level 5 response	**Why the pupils achieved a Level 5**
*Alan Sugar thinks more should be done to stop youth crime **and he wants the reader to agree with him.** "If it were up to me I'd use a sledgehammer to crack a nut. The Government needs to invest more money in the police force." This would make the reader feel like more should be done to stop youth crime.*	*Main purpose clearly identified through general overview.* *Limited explanation of viewpoint.* *General awareness of the effect on the reader.*

How could we move this response into Level 6?

- More precise use of evidence
- Developed explanation of viewpoint
- Explanation of how the effect has been created

What is needed to make the next step?

One of the most effective techniques to use when helping to progress to level 6+ in AF6 reading is to ensure that the evidence (quotations/layout features/language devices) you use directly supports your point of view. It is also vital that you are aware of what tools a writer is using to achieve the effect on the reader.

For example:

AF6 – Level 5 response	AF6 – Level 6 response
Alan Sugar thinks more should be done to stop youth crime and he wants the reader to agree with him. "If it were up to me I'd use a sledgehammer to crack a nut. The Government needs to invest more money in the police force." This would make the reader feel like more should be done to stop youth crime.	*Alan Sugar thinks more should be done to stop youth crime and he forcefully argues this case to the reader "If it were up to me I'd use a sledgehammer to crack a nut." He uses this metaphor to illustrate his view that a more aggressive approach to dealing with youth crime is needed. He is raising the issue with the public as well as pleading with the government to take more action.*

Notice how the Level 6 response comments on how the viewpoint is shown (forcefully) as well as how the effect has been created (metaphor) on the audience.

AF6 Progress Challenge C

Read through the extract below and the responses that are given to the task set. What advice (and alternative answers) would you give to the students who came up with these responses for them to achieve a Level 6?

How does Sir Alan effectively communicate his views on youth crime in this extract?

> Sir Alan, who grew up on a tough council estate in East London, offered troublemakers an olive branch by urging ministers to invest in community projects and youth centres "where kids can go and feel good about themselves."
>
> He said: *"We need to work with hoodies to understand them better, to find out why they've chosen the route they have. It's a flaw in the education system so maybe it's hard for this to happen at schools."*
> *"We need to employ people to give them somewhere to go. Eventually some might get off their backsides and get a job."*

Pupil responses to this question:

He wants to give the youths an olive branch

He wants kids to feel good about themselves

He thinks that education is rubbish which is why kids kick off and get into trouble

He wishes that kids would get off their bums and help themselves

Next steps…

Look through your previous work on responding to a reading question and check whether you have always:

- used precise quotations that explicitly support your points
- explained the viewpoint of the writer
- explained how an effect on the reader has been created.

Progress Checker D – (Level 6-7 reading progression)

	AF6 – Identify and comment on writers' purposes and viewpoints, and the overall effect of the text on the reader.	
I	What level am I currently working at in AF6 reading?	Level 6
	What skills do I currently have in this assessment focus?	As a Level 6 reader in AF6 I am able to: • identify the main purpose of the text through using evidence precisely. • clearly identify and explain a writers' viewpoint through close reference to the text • explicitly explain how effects have been created on the reader
	What skills do I need to develop to reach the next level?	To be a confident AF7 reader at Level 6 I need to • analyse and evaluate the author's purpose • analyse and evaluate how a viewpoint is managed in a text • show appreciation for how devices and effects achieve the effects they do

Moving a Level 6 response to Level 7

In order to progress to level 7 in this assessment focus you need to begin to question the author's purpose and viewpoint (not just identify it) For example, what other motivations may Sir Alan Sugar have in writing his article on youth crime? Could it be for self interest or because he likes the publicity or is it because he genuinely wants to raise the issue with the public?

You also need to consider the effectiveness of the devices used by a writer. For example, when Sir Alan says "We need to work with hoodies to understand them better" he is purposely using street language in order for the public to see that he can identify with young people. He is also using the word 'We' which creates the sense that 'we' the public are united in his view.

Read through the task and the example below. Look at how this pupil has achieved level 6 and think about what they could do to improve.

In this extract how does The Sun try and convince its readers to accept their opinions?

> The Government must respond, too. And quickly, for there is not a moment to lose. Five months ago Prime Minister Gordon Brown promised The Sun a crackdown on knife crime in a dozen "hotspots" around Britain. Today he must extend it nationwide. The Sun also demands automatic PROSECUTION for those caught with a knife, and an immediate end to them getting away with just a police caution.

AF6 – Level 6 response	Why the pupils achieved a Level 6
'The Sun' uses aggressive language and instructions to convince its audience of its point of view. Words such as "must" and "demand" are orders which the reader would be happy to see the government take out to help reduce youth crime	Evidence used to show understanding of purpose and viewpoint Effect on the reader explained

How could we move this response into Level 7?

This response needs to be more evaluative in its use of evidence, and begin questioning the purpose and viewpoint in greater detail. For example, as well as revealing its views on youth crime, it is important to remember that **The Sun** has another important agenda to meet – keeping its readership happy. This response also needs to consider how successfully the techniques used by **The Sun** will impact on its audience.

What is needed to make the next step?

One of the most effective techniques to use when helping to progress to level 7+ in AF6 reading is to ensure that for every reference you make to the question set and the points you make, it is important to question and challenge the viewpoints of the author as well as considering how the effects have been created and in what ways would a reader be affected by them.

For example.

AF6 – Level 6 response	AF6 – Level 7 response
'The Sun' uses aggressive language and instructions to convince its audience of its point of view. Words such as "must" and "demand" are orders which the reader would be happy to see the government take out to help reduce youth crime.	'The Sun' uses aggressive language in an attempt to identify with the public who will feel outraged and deeply concerned with the increase in youth crime. It's approach would likely have a significant impact on its readers (and hopefully new readers), particularly how it clearly wants to take the moral high ground "Gordon Brown promised 'The Sun'" creates the impression on the reader that their views are being listened to in high places.

Notice how the Level 7 response begins to analyse the motivations that **The Sun** has in presenting its article as it does. It also begins evaluating the effects that may be created on its audience.

AF6 Progress Challenge D

Look at the following text and analyse the possible motivations for this being produced. Comment also on the possible effects on the target audience.

Sir Alan Sugar's dismay at 'BROKEN BRITAIN'
By Sam Wilson

Sir Alan Sugar has criticised the state of modern Britain and called for billions of pounds to be invested in the police force to tackle yob culture.

Speaking exclusively to The Sun newspaper, the Amstrad tycoon, 61, demanded "radical" investment from the Government to put thousands more police on the streets.

The Apprentice guru, thought to be worth £880 million, also urged youngsters to use their initiative to achieve success in business, craft, or sport rather than relying on state handouts.

1) Analysis of possible motivations
2) Effects on the target audience

Next steps… When reading a text in class or at home, consider the alternative motivations that the author may have in producing this text. Put yourself in the shoes of the target audience (not yourself necessarily) and begin analysing the differing effects that may (or may not) have been created on you. What could the author have done differently to have a greater impact on you?

What strategies could I use to progress further?

Programme of Study Links	**Creativity** - using inventive approaches to making meaning. **Cultural understanding** - gaining a sense of the English literary heritage.
Framework Objectives	**Understanding author's craft** - relating texts to the social, historical and cultural contexts in which they were written. Using different dramatic approaches to explore ideas, texts and issues
Personal Learning & Thinking Skills	**Enquiry** - asking questions, predict outcomes and anticipate consequences. **Evaluation** - judging the value of what is read and personally written.
AFL	Exploration of success criteria. Examining effective feedback.
Assessment Focus	**AF3:** - deduce, infer or interpret information, events or ideas from a text.
Functional Skills	Detecting point of view. Writing for a real context.

Challenge 1- Get thinking

What has helped me learn effectively today?

a) From which play do you think these images are from?
b) How did you come to your decision?

a) Much Ado
   About Nothing
b) Richard III
c) The Tempest
d) Macbeth

Below is an overview of how you will develop your skills as an effective and critical reader in this unit.

In this unit I will learn how to effectively…
(Learning Objectives)

Understand author's craft – relating texts to the social, historical and cultural contexts in which they were written.

The topics I will be studying are…
(Stimulus)

Extracts from:

Macbeth/Richard III
Much Ado About Nothing/ The Tempest

My understand will be checked by seeing how I…
(Assessment Criteria)

Deduce, infer or interpret information, events or ideas from a text. (AF3)

My achievement will be demonstrated through me successfully completing the following challenges:
(Learning Outcomes)

Challenge 1	Get thinking – image response
Challenge 2	KWL
Challenge 3	Summary analysis
Challenge 4	Word speculation
Challenge 5	Banquo character study
Challenge 6	Question choices
Challenge 7	Emotions of Banquo and Macbeth
Challenge 8	Soliloquy response
Challenge 9	Structured response to Macbeth
Challenge 10	Word headache
Challenge 11	Drama techniques
Challenge 12	Adjective response
Challenge 13	Marking a written response
Challenge 14	Comical paragraph
Challenge 15	Language analysis of Richard III
Challenge 16	Improve an exemplar response
Challenge 17	Group organisation
Challenge 18	Pupil choices
Challenge 19	Beatrice language analysis
Challenge 20	2 sentence task
Challenge 21	Decisions, decisions
Challenge 22	Close task
Challenge 23	Glossary game
Challenge 24	Traffic lights
Challenge 25	Sculpture
Challenge 26	KWL complete
	Future Skills

In this chapter, you will be exploring how you can identify with Shakespeare's:

- ideas
- characters
- language
- stage

Why is it important to still explore Shakespeare?

As well as exploring the points above, this chapter will also demonstrate how Shakespeare is extremely relevant and influential to modern writers and film makers.

So what will I gain from doing this?

By the end of this chapter you will have a deeper understanding of how characters and ideas are communicated effectively through language and performance; this should develop you as an effective:

- reader (as you analyse the language devices of Shakespeare and their effects on the audience)
- writer (as you experiment with interpreting and adapting some of Shakespeare's language devices for your own writing)
- director/actor (as you explore the way Shakespeare uses the stage to achieve particular dramatic effects)

How many plays am I expected to read?

Will I have to read the whole play?

In this chapter you will be focusing on particular scenes from Shakespeare's plays which are effective examples of how character, ideas, language and performance are communicated to the audience. You will need to understand the overall plot of each play and your teacher may wish for you to explore a whole play in depth, so you can get an even deeper understanding of Shakespeare's techniques and relevance to you. The scenes that we will be exploring are from the following plays, some of which you may be familiar with.

    Macbeth
    Richard III
    Much Ado About Nothing
    The Tempest

As a quick opener, discuss the following headings with your learning partner and complete the first two columns (Know & Want)

	Know What do I already know about this play?	**Want** What do I want to find out? (think about the introduction of this chapter)	**Learnt** What have I now learnt from this chapter that I didn't previously know?
Macbeth			
Richard III			
The Tempest			
Much Ado About Nothing			

You will have an opportunity to complete the Learnt section at the end of this chapter.

Challenge 3

You now need to find a summary of each play (your teacher will have a version if you cannot find one). You will probably notice that the information is presented in a very dull and uninteresting way. Divide yourselves into the four plays (there may be more than one group per play, depending on the size).

In your group, you need to complete the following:

a) Read through a summary of your play
b) Choose either an image or a phrase which sums up the main action in each scene
c) Test out your summary sheet by seeing whether another group can tell which scene you are referring to. You could do a family tree or a RIP/Body count.
d) Produce a quiz on each play which will test whether the rest of the class have understood the plot.

Exploring character

In this section we will be exploring how Shakespeare communicates his characters':

- goals/hopes/fears
- relationship with others
- actions
- emotional development/change

Have you ever let your... Heart rule your head? Mouth run away with you?

In other words, there must have been occasions where what you have said, is not necessarily that close to being either what's in your heart (your feelings/emotions/instincts) and your head (what your mind is telling you – your rational, more considered/thoughtful side).

This is also true of Macbeth and Banquo in this scene as they are both very careful to disguise what their real concerns and feelings are, for fear of their plans being exposed and realised, resulting in their hopes being dashed.

For this challenge, you need to carefully consider what Macbeth & Banquo are saying, compared to what they thinking and feeling. Some examples have been completed for you.

Challenge 7

In what other subjects could I apply these skills?

BANQUO   **MACBETH**

> All's well. I dreamt last night of the three weird sisters: To you they have show'd some truth.

> I think not of them: Yet, when we can entreat an hour to serve, We would spend it in some words upon that business, If you would grant the time.

> I need to work out how ambitious he is – what is he prepared to do?

> I need to check whether Banquo will support me

> I am frightened of this man who I thought was my friend. I care about him though can I trust him?

> I want rid of him now – he's in my way

Once Banquo leaves, Macbeth delivers his famous soliloquy (a speech delivered by an actor alone on stage), in which he reveals his inner torment, shown by the image of a blood-stained dagger leading him to Duncan's door.

Act 2, scene 1
Macbeth's soliloquy

Context	Glossary
• Macbeth cannot decide whether the dagger is real or simply a vision from his 'heat-oppressed' brain. • He questions whether his eyes are playing tricks on his other senses. • He already has fears of his sleep being disturbed by wicked dreams. • He compares his stalking of Duncan to the actions of a Roman rapist, Tarquin. • He compares the howl of a wolf to the signal that Lady Macbeth will give him before Duncan's murder. • The bell rings and Macbeth goes towards Duncan's chamber to murder him.	**So I lose none** **In seeking to augment it, but still keep** **My bosom franchised and allegiance clear,** **I shall be counsell'd.** I will be loyal to you as long as it does not make me dishonourable. **have thee not**: unable to grab you **heat-oppresed**: hot, feverish **palpable**: real/touchable **marshall'st**: direct **Mine eyes are made the fools o' the other senses,** **Or else worth all the rest** My eyes are playing tricks on me or are working better than my other senses. **Hecate**: goddess of witchcraft **Alarum'd**: called into action **sentinel**: watchman **Tarquin**: a Roman rapist **knell**: funeral bell

In groups of 5 (A,B,C,D,E), read through Macbeth's soliloquy and complete the following:
a) choose one image and word which most effectively represents each section
b) as you read the line produce a physical representation (gesture) of this image and word
c) test other groups to see if they can guess the correct line from your image/gesture

Group A	Is this a dagger which I see before me, The handle toward my hand? Come, let me clutch thee: I have thee not, and yet I see thee still. Art thou not, fatal vision, sensible To feeling, as to sight? or art thou but A dagger of the mind, a false creation, Proceeding from the heat-oppressed brain? I see thee yet, in form as palpable As this which now I draw. Thou marshall'st me the way that I was going; And such an instrument I was to use.	35 40
Group B	Mine eyes are made the fools o' the other senses, Or else worth all the rest: I see thee still; And on thy blade, and dudgeon, gouts of blood, Which was not so before. There's no such thing. It is the bloody business which informs Thus to mine eyes.	45
Group C	Now o'er the one half-world Nature seems dead, and wicked dreams abuse. The curtain'd sleep: witchcraft celebrates Pale Hecate's offerings; and wither'd murder, alarum'd by his sentinel, the wolf, Whose howl's his watch, thus with his stealthy pace. With Tarquin's ravishing strides, towards his design Moves like a ghost.	50 55
Group D	Thou sure and firm-set earth, Hear not my steps, which way they walk, for fear Thy very stones prate of my where-about, And take the present horror from the time, Which now suits with it. Whiles I threat, he lives: Words to the heat of deeds too cold breath gives.	60
Group E	A bell rings. I go, and it is done: the bell invites me. Hear it not, Duncan; for it is a knell That summons thee to heaven, or to hell.	 Exit

Writing an extended answer on character

Question: Explore how Banquo's character is presented in Act 2, Scene I.

Steps	Sequence of a writing response	Example
I	Make your point	*Banquo is revealed as being on edge in this scene.*
2	Use evidence	*"Give me my sword." "Who's there?"*
3	Explain the significance of this point	*This demonstrates Banquo's anxious frame of mind, which has been caused by the Witches' prophecies.*
4	Comment on the intended effect on the audience	*The audience would feel sympathy for Banquo's situation, especially as his son would appear to be in grave danger in view of the Witches' earlier prediction that Banquo will "get kings". This suggests that Fleance will be a future barrier to Macbeth's legacy.*

Challenge 9

Using this structure, answer the following question:

What does the audience discover about Macbeth's state of mind from his soliloquy?

Steps	Sequence of a writing response	Example
I	Make your point	
2	Use evidence	
3	Explain the significance of this point	
4	Comment on the intended effect on the audience	

What has helped me learn effectively today?

Before we look at the next scene, give yourself a headache by looking at the list of words below which have been jumbled together from Act 2, scene 2.

a) As a pair, look through this list and pick out the 20 most interesting words
b) Using **these words only**, create a short poem
c) Explain how you came to make your decision.

address'd, afraid, Amen, attempt, awak'd, balm, bellman, bleed, bless, blessing, blood, bold, brainsickly, care, castle, Cawdor, chamber, charge, clean, clears, chief, colour, confounds, consider, constancy, contend, could, crickets, cried, cry, daggers, dare, dead, death, deeds, deeply, descended, Devil, did, don't, doors, drugg'd, drunk, Duncan, enter, eyes, faces, fatal, father, fears, feast, filthy, fire, foolish, get, gild, give, Glamis, go, God, goodnight, green, grooms, guilt, HA!, hands, hangman's, Hark!, hath, heard, hear, his, ho!, house, how, hurt, husband, in, incarnadine, innocent, knits, knocking, know, lady, laid, laugh, lie, life, listening, little, live, lodged, look, lost, Macbeth, mad, making, me, mean, minds, mine, miss, mock, more, most, multitudinous, murder, murder'd, must, my, myself, nature's, need, Neptune's, nightgown, noble, noise, nourisher, occasion, ocean, one, open, our, out, owl, painted, peace, pictures, place, pluck, poorly, possets, prayers, pronounce, purpose, rather, ready, red, resembled, retire, say, scream, second, seem, shall, shame, show, shriek'd, sight, sleep, sleeve, slept, smear, snores, so, some, sore, sorry, south, speak, stood, strength, stuck, surfeited, thane, the, their, them, then, there, therefore, these, they, things, think, this, thou, thoughts, throat, thus, thy, together, to, two, unattended, unbend, up, us, voice, wake, wash, watchers, water, we, wear, what, when, wherefore, whether, which, white, why, will, with, withal, within, witness, worthy, would, you, your

Exploring character through performance

In the following extract, Macbeth returns to his wife, having murdered Duncan.
In pairs, take on the roles of Macbeth and Lady Macbeth as they discuss what to do next. Practice some of the dramatic techniques below when reading out the lines and think about the different effects created.

- whisper/shout certain words
- use gestures for each line which reveals your character's thoughts and feelings
- vary the tone you deliver your lines; i.e. sarcastic, fearful, sly, angry etc.
- vary how long you take to respond to the other character; i.e. pausing for 5 seconds or responding immediately before they have a chance to fully finish their line
- before you read out your line, select a word or phrase from the other character's speech and say that before reading your own.

For example:

> **MACBETH**   I have done the deed. Didst thou not hear a noise?
>
> **LADY**   (the deed!) I heard the owl scream, and the crickets cry.
> **MACBETH**

Act 2, Scene II   Macbeth's castle
Enter LADY MACBETH.

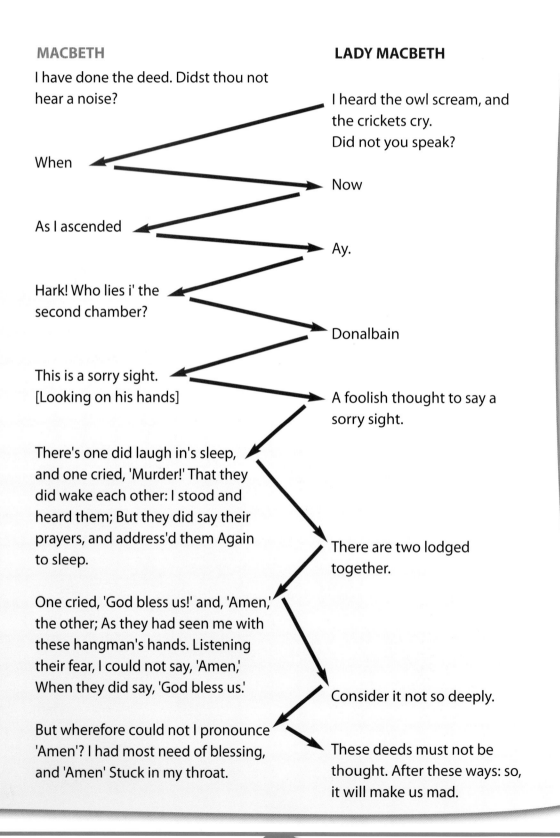

MACBETH

I have done the deed. Didst thou not hear a noise?

When

As I ascended

Hark! Who lies i' the second chamber?

This is a sorry sight.
[Looking on his hands]

There's one did laugh in's sleep, and one cried, 'Murder!' That they did wake each other: I stood and heard them; But they did say their prayers, and address'd them Again to sleep.

One cried, 'God bless us!' and, 'Amen,' the other; As they had seen me with these hangman's hands. Listening their fear, I could not say, 'Amen,' When they did say, 'God bless us.'

But wherefore could not I pronounce 'Amen'? I had most need of blessing, and 'Amen' Stuck in my throat.

LADY MACBETH

I heard the owl scream, and the crickets cry.
Did not you speak?

Now

Ay.

Donalbain

A foolish thought to say a sorry sight.

There are two lodged together.

Consider it not so deeply.

These deeds must not be thought. After these ways: so, it will make us mad.

The following extracts are from near the end of the play (Act 5, scenes III & V) which sees Macbeth is in his castle, awaiting the attack of Malcolm and Macduff.

Consider an adjective to describe Macbeth during these lines. Use some of the phrases below in your answer

Shakespeare – shows, reveals, reflects, implies, reinforces, represents, echoes, indicates, demonstrates, symbolises, epitomises

Bring me no more reports; let them fly all

I am sick at heart,

Our castle's strength Will laugh a siege to scorn

I'll fight, till from my bones my flesh be hack'd.

Give me my armour

Canst thou not minister to a mind diseased

I have almost forgot the taste of tears

I have supped full of horrors

She should have died heareafter

Out! Out, brief candle!

Life is but a walking shadow

At least we'll die with harness on our back.

Writing an extended answer on character

Read through the responses below and make 3 positive observations, whilst including one target for improvement.

How does Shakespeare want his audience to respond to Macbeth at this point in the play?

Steps	Sequence of a writing response	Example	
1	Make your point	Macbeth's sense of desperation has clearly increased in this scene.	Shakespeare presents Macbeth as a tragic and desperate figure who has lost touch with humanity in this scene. When he hears the cry of a woman he says…"
2	Use evidence	"Bring me no more reports; let them fly all"	"I have almost forgot the taste of tears."
3	Explain the significance of this point	He can no longer cope with hearing the news of his impending doom and instead decides to dismiss the fact that he is being deserted.	This epitomises the deterioration of Macbeth's character. Once a man of integrity and honour, the "horrors" that he has "supp'd full" with memories are of have stripped all sense of decency and empathy.
4	Comment on the intended effect on the audience	The audience would feel torn between their sympathy and respect for Macbeth at this point in the play; his refusal to face up to his predicament reveals his deterioration and vulnerability. Although aware of his murderous reign, the audience could not help to admire his courage and defiance in the face of such adversity.	Shakespeare wants the audience to view Macbeth as a tragic figure who is not without admirable qualities. It is because of Macbeth's self-realisation that we sympathise with his character, in spite of the evil acts he has performed.

Exploring language

In this section we will be considering how Shakespeare uses language imaginatively to convey the emotions of the characters and reflect the mood and atmosphere of the scene.

Shakespeare's use of Language Prompts for Exploration
What particular language devices are used? • Symbolism • Metaphor? • Variation in prose/ verse (often to signify status and mood change) • Alliteration • Rhyming couplets • Dramatic irony • Double meaning • Powerful verbs/adjectives/adverbs/abstract nouns • Invented words/insults
What is the effect of the language on the audience? **What mood is created?** • Increases pace of the action • Reinforces our understanding of character • Darken/lighten the mood • Create tension • Excitement/anticipation
What does the language used reveal about changes/developments in character? • Deterioration (i.e. Macbeth) • Increased confidence
How do the language choices communicate the cultural significance of the play • Use of spells in Macbeth to communicate belief in witchcraft
What do the language choices reveal about Shakespeare's beliefs and writing purposes? • To support the monarchy (James 1st, Macbeth) • To reveal the temporary nature of love (Romeo & Juliet)

Below is a list of famous sayings from Shakespeare's work, the majority of which, he invented. In pairs, read through this list, select 10 examples to create a comical description.

- All's well that ends well
- Bated breath
- Bear a charmed life
- Be-all and the end-all
- Brave new world
- Break the ice
- Breathed his last
- Refuse to budge an inch
- Cold comfort
- Crack of doom
- Devil incarnate
- Eaten me out of house and home
- Faint hearted Fancy-free
- Fool's paradise
- Forever and a day
- For goodness' sake
- Foregone conclusion
- Full circle
- The game is up
- Good riddance
- Green-eyed monster
- Heart of gold
- In a pickle
- In my heart of hearts
- In my mind's eye
- Kill with kindness
- Laid on with a trowel
- Laughing stock
- Lean and hungry look
- Lie low
- Love is blind
- Melted into thin air
- Murder most foul
- Murder will out
- Naked truth

- Neither rhyme nor reason
- Not slept a wink
- Once more into the breach
- One fell swoop
- Out of the jaws of death
- Own flesh and blood
- Star-crossed lovers
- A plague on both your houses
- Play fast and loose
- Pound of flesh
- Sea change
- Seen better days
- Send packing
- Make short shrift
- Sick at heart
- Snail paced
- Something wicked this way comes
- A sorry sight
- Sound and fury
- Spotless reputation
- Stony hearted
- Such stuff as dreams are made on
- Set my teeth on edge
- There's the rub
- This mortal coil
- Too much of a good thing
- Tower of strength
- Truth will out
- Wear my heart upon my sleeve
- What's done is done
- Wild-goose chase

Using the language of manipulation

Manipulation: to control or influence somebody or something in a clever or devious way.

In this scene from Richard III, the Duke of York (Richard) wants to get rid of a popular nobleman, Hastings, as he suspects he will stand between his evil plans to become King. Richard knows that Hastings is having an affair with Shore's wife and exploits this vulnerability by publically accusing her of witchcraft; this tricks Hastings into doubting the accusation, which Richard purposely interprets as him being disloyal.

Challenge 15

As you read through this exchange, pick out the verbs and adjectives used by Richard to exert his authority and manipulate those around him.

In what other subjects could I apply these skills?

Act 3, Scene 4 (58-end)
Re-enter RICHARD and BUCKINGHAM

RICHARD	I pray you all, tell me what they deserve	
	That do conspire my death with devilish plots	
	Of damnéd witchcraft, and that have prevailed	60
	Upon my body with their hellish charms?	
HASTINGS	The tender love I bear your Grace, my lord,	
	Makes me most forward in this noble presence	
	To doom th' offenders, whosoe'er they be.	
	I say, my lord, they have deservéd death.	65
RICHARD	Then be your eyes the witness of their evil.	
	Look how I am bewitched! Behold, mine arm	
	Is like a blasted sapling withered up!	
	And this is Edward's wife, that monstrous witch,	
	Consorted with that harlot strumpet Shore,	70
	That by their witchcraft thus have markéd me.	
HASTINGS	If they have done this deed, my noble lord—	
RICHARD	If? - Thou protector of this damnéd strumpet!	
	Talk'st thou to me of ifs? Thou art a traitor!	
	Off with his head! Now by Saint Paul I swear,	75
	I will not dine until I see the same.	
	Lovell and Ratcliffe, look that it be done.	
	The rest that love me, rise and follow me.	

Exit RICHARD. All follow, except HASTINGS, RATCLIFFE, and LOVELL

Read through the response below which explores how Shakespeare uses language to reveal Richard's manipulative side. Which aspects of the response do you feel you could incorporate into your own written response?

> *This extract is dominated by Richard's intimidating, aggressive and extremely powerful use of language, which terrifies those around him into submission. Shakespeare uses alliteration in the opening lines, "deserve, death, devilish", in order to create the mood*
> *of evil and tension, as well as revealing Richard's ability as a dramatic and persuasive speaker.*
>
> *Moreover, Shakespeare uses powerful verbs - "conspire" "consorted" - as well as the effective simile, "mine arm is like a blasted sapling", to give Richard's performance greater edge, conviction and ultimately, reward (Hastings' death). Richard is intentionally vague in his opening rhetorical questions, refusing to name the supposed conspirators*
> *in order to entice Hastings; Richard exploits the simple phrase 'if' as justification for the beheading of Hastings. By the end of this extract, Richard is in complete command, demonstrated by his imperative "look that it be done" and his ultimatum, "the rest that love me, rise and follow me".*

After the beheading of Hastings, Richard is aware that the news of Hastings' death will cause uproar amongst the citizens, especially the Mayor, as Hastings was a well loved and respected noble. In order to justify their actions, Richard and Buckingham decide to play act, putting on old armour in order to suggest that they are in fear for their lives.

As you read through this extract, consider how Richard uses languages dramatically to achieve his aim of convincing the public (and the mayor in particular) that it was right for Hastings to be killed.

RICHARD	Look to the drawbridge there!	15
BUCKINGHAM	Hark! A drum.	
RICHARD	Catesby, o'erlook the walls!	
BUCKINGHAM	Lord Mayor, the reason we have sent -	
RICHARD	Look back, defend thee! Here are enemies!	
BUCKINGHAM	God and our innocence defend and guard us!	20
LOVELL	Here is the head of that ignoble traitor, The dangerous and unsuspected Hastings.	
RICHARD	So dear I loved the man that I must weep.	
	I took him for the plainest harmless creature	25
	That breathed upon the earth a Christian:	
	Made him my book, wherein my soul recorded	
	The history of all her secret thoughts.	
	So smooth he daubed his vice with show of virtue	
	That, his apparent open guilt omitted -	30
	I mean his conversation with Shore's wife -	
	He lived from all attainder of suspects.	
BUCKINGHAM	Well, well, he was the covert'st sheltered traitor	
	That ever lived!	
	Would you imagine, or almost believe -	35
	Were't not that by great preservation	
	We live to tell it - that the subtle traitor	
	This day had plotted, in the council-house,	
	To murder me and my good Lord of Gloucester?	
MAYOR	Had he done so?	40
RICHARD	What! Think you we are Turks or infidels?	
	Or that we would, against the form of law,	
	Proceed thus rashly in the villain's death,	
	But that the extreme peril of the case,	
	The peace of England and our persons' safety,	45
	Enforced us to this execution?	
MAYOR	Now fair befall you! He deserved his death!	
	And you my good Graces both have well proceeded	
	To warn false traitors from the like attempts.	

In a small group, read through the questions below. Between you, organise yourselves so that all 10 questions are completed

1. When the Mayor arrives, Shakespeare decides to shorten the line length. What impact does this have on the atmosphere?
2. What is the intention of Richard and Buckingham when they pretend that they are afraid?
3. What was Shakespeare's purpose in bringing in the 'head' of Hastings.
4. How would the other characters in the scene react to this horrific sight?
5. Richard decides to initially show apparent sadness at the death of Hastings. What phrases does he use and what are his intentions here?
6. How does the Mayor initially respond to hearing the news of Hastings' apparent treachery?
7. Comment on the language used by Richard in responding to the doubts of the Mayor.
8. Buckingham tries to divert blame from Richard on the speed that Hastings was murdered. How does he argue this point across to the Mayor?
9. Why are Richard and Buckingham determined that the Mayor shall inform the citizens of the justifications of Hastings' murder?
10. What are the audience expected to feel at this point in the play?

Writing an extended response on language

Challenge 18

Read through the table below.

What other choices could the pupil have made when coming up with this response How does Shakespeare use language to reveal the manipulative nature of Richard?

Steps	Sequence of a writing response	Example
1	Make your point	*Richard is shown to have many powers of manipulation in these scenes, particularly when he puts on a dramatic performance in front of the Mayor in order to justify Hastings' murder.*
2	Use evidence	*"So dear I loved the man that I must weep."*
3	Explain the significance of this point	*Shakespeare presents the sly and cunning nature of Richard. His use of the words "So dear" is dramatically ironic as the audience have knowledge of Richard's evil intentions to rid Hastings from his path to the throne.*
4	Comment on the intended effect on the audience	*Even though the audience would find Richard's deception disturbing, they could not help but admire his sheer brash confidence and use of melodrama.*

Exploring themes, issues and ideas

When responding to Shakespeare it is important to reflect on how

- the important issues of the time were communicated to his audience;
- his experiences shaped his writing through the way he chose to adapt and interpret history for his own purpose;
- his exploration of challenging issues are timeless – they are still as relevant for a modern audience.

Ideas, themes and issues
Prompts for exploration

What are the prominent themes? i.e.:
- War / Power / Paralysis / Entrapment / Fate / Ambition
- Kingship / Evil / Revenge / Corruption / Relationships

How are the themes presented to the audience? i.e:
- through the character's actions
- their words
- their body language
- stage directions
- what other characters say about them
- use of symbols

What social events and beliefs may have shaped and influenced Shakespeare's writing? i.e.
- Monarchy rule
- Witchcraft
- Religious beliefs
- Roles of men and women

In what ways are the issues Shakespeare explored, still relevant today. i.e:
- purpose of war
- roles of men & women
- power and control
- corruption
- conflicts between religions

In the next scene from **Much Ado about Nothing**, Beatrice is deeply upset that her cousin, Hero has been falsely accused of being unfaithful to her husband to be, Claudio, who has just publically humiliated her by dumping her at the alter. Beatrice and Benedick, after a long feud throughout the play, have finally admitted their love for each other and Beatrice wants Benedick to prove his devotion by killing Claudio (who is his closet friend)

Cultural relevance?

- How many soaps have you seen where someone is dramatically dumped at the alter for (allegedly) being unfaithful?
- How many films have you watched where a woman is trying to get a man to do something for her in order to prove his love? (and the other way round too.)
- How many stories have you read where someone is put in a seemingly impossible position and felt torn?
- How many times have you heard a discussion about the rights of women?

As well as the interest in character, the following scene explores the role of women.

Challenge 19

What do you feel these phrases might suggest about Beatrice?

- O that I were a man!
- God, that I were a man! I would eat his heart in the market-place
- That I were a man for his sake! or that I had any friend would be a man for my sake!
- But manhood is melted into courtesies, valour into compliment, and men are only turned into tongue, and trim ones too:
- I cannot be a man with wishing, therefore I will die a woman with grieving.

In what other subjects could I apply these skills?

Read through the scene and complete the following two sentences:

1) Shakespeare's beliefs on the role of women in society are _____

_____

2) It has cultural relevance because _____

_____

BENEDICK	Come, bid me do any thing for thee.	
BEATRICE	Kill Claudio.	
BENEDICK	Ha! not for the wide world.	
BEATRICE	You kill me to deny it. Farewell.	285
BENEDICK	Tarry, sweet Beatrice.	
BEATRICE	I am gone, though I am here: there is no love in you Nay, I pray you, let me go.	
BENEDICK	Beatrice,	
BEATRICE	In faith, I will go.	290
BENEDICK	We'll be friends first.	
BEATRICE	You dare easier be friends with me than fight with mine enemy.	
BENEDICK	Is Claudio thine enemy?	
BEATRICE	Is he not approved in the height a villain, that hath slandered, scorned, dishonoured my kinswoman? O that I were a man! What, bear her in hand until they come to take hands; and then, with public accusation, uncovered slander, unmitigated rancour - O God, that I were a man! I would eat his heart in the market-place.	295 300
BENEDICK	Hear me, Beatrice	
BEATRICE	Talk with a man out at a window! A proper saying!	
BENEDICK	Nay, but, Beatrice,	
BEATRICE	Sweet Hero! She is wronged, she is slandered, she Is undone.	305
BENEDICK	Beat	
BEATRICE	Princes and counties! Surely, a princely testimony, a goodly count, Count Comfect; a sweet gallant, surely! O that I were a man for his sake! or that I had any friend would be a man for my sake! But manhood is melted into courtesies, valour into compliment, and men are only turned into tongue, and trim ones too: he is now as valiant as Hercules that only tells a lie and swears it. I cannot be a man with wishing, therefore I will die a woman with grieving.	 310 315
BENEDICK	Tarry, good Beatrice. By this hand, I love thee.	
BEATRICE	Use it for my love some other way than swearing by it.	
BENEDICK	Think you in your soul the Count Claudio hath wronged Hero?	
BEATRICE	Yea, as sure as I have a thought or a soul.	320

What has helped me learn effectively today?

Steps	Sequence of a writing response	Example
1	Make your point	Beatrice is revealed as being _____ to her cousin, _____ and _____ at the role of women in her society. This vulnerability and _____ for a saviour is shown in the way she _____ to Benedick asking her how a _____ may help her.
2	Use evidence	"It is a man's office, but not _____"
3	Explain the significance of this point	Shakespeare presents _____ as being fully aware of a woman's role in that society, though he allows her to retain some _____ over proceedings by her persuasion of Benedick to stand up for her. This reveals Beatrice's need for reassurance and her inner conflict of Benedick as her lover and trying to maintain her _____ and fiery spirit.
4	Comment on the intended effect on the audience	Shakespeare's _____ would _____ with her deep upset, admire her attempts to remain independent whilst being aware that within that society it was a _____ 'office' to deal with such conflict.

Challenge 22

When could I use these skills outside of school?

Read through the exemplar response and discuss what the missing words might be (you could use the choice here or your own)

Accepting, audience, Beatrice, conflict control, frustrated, independent, loyal man, man's, pleading, responds saviour, subtle, sympathise, vulnerable, yours

Exploring Shakespeare's text in performance

Text in performance
Prompts for exploration

As you know, Shakespeare's text was (and still is) expected to be performed, rather than to be simply read.

When considering how to explore the stage and performance there are two key questions:

1) What advice would you give to an actor playing a character?
2) How would you direct these scenes?

This is so the full power of Shakespeare's language, themes and character can be realised and fully appreciated by the audience.

Remember to explain how your decisions as a director would help to communicate the following to a Shakespearian audience:

- the personality, behaviour and the inner relationships of the characters
- the atmosphere and mood of the scene
- the themes that are most evident in the scene

Atmosphere
How could the following be used to create the desired atmosphere?
the organisation of the stage: props; lighting; spot lights; fog; music/sound effects/ use of levels

Characterisation
How would you communicate the relationships between the characters as well as their individual feelings and actions?
costume; tone of voice; body language; position and movement of characters; emphasis of key words and phrases.

Advice to the actor(s)
Consider how they should communicate their feelings to:
themselves; the other characters; the audience.

Tempestuous Thinking

The speech we are looking at to explore performance is near the end of The Tempest when Prospero calls up his magic helpers, the elves and fairies and his low-ranking spirits in order to inform them, and the audience, that he now wishes to bury his staff, his magic book and all the powers that comes with it. He reflects with affection and a touch of sadness his feats in being able to raise the tempest and control the sea and sky through his all-mighty power. Prospero also refers to previous magic and describes some of his skills as 'rough' which implies they are merely magic tricks.

As a quick way in to the scene and some of the complex language and images that are created, see if you can match the following list of key words from the soliloquy with the correct definition

Glossary	
Elves	receding Tide
Printless foot	Prospero is referring to the spirits who have lower rank and status
Ebbing Neptune	previous magic tricks
Demi-puppets –	to drop steeply and suddenly downwards
Green sour ringlets	creatures unable to make a foot print (because they are invisible)
Curfew	the oak tree was sacred to Jove (the God of thunder and lightening)
Weak masters	measurement of man's outstretched arms
Twixt the green sea and the azured vault Set roaring war –	mischievous creatures of magic
Rifted	renounce/reject
Jove 's stout oak	split
Spurs	rings in the grass caused by dancing fairies
Graves	roots
Rough magic	the nine-o'clock evening bell
Abjure	magic that is in the air
Mine end	unsophisticated/visible/magic tricks
Airy charm	my purpose
Fathom	Prospero describes his elves as being like puppets or dolls that he can control
Plummet	reference to prospero's creation of the tempest.

Ye elves of hills, brooks, standing lakes and groves,
And ye that on the sands with printless foot
Do chase the ebbing Neptune and do fly him
When he comes back; you demi-puppets that
By moonshine do the green sour ringlets make,
Whereof the ewe not bites, and you whose pastime
Is to make midnight mushrooms, that rejoice
To hear the solemn curfew; by whose aid,
Weak masters though ye be, I have bedimm'd
The noontide sun, call'd forth the mutinous winds,
And 'twixt the green sea and the azured vault
Set roaring war: to the dread rattling thunder
Have I given fire and rifted Jove's stout oak
With his own bolt; the strong-based promontory
Have I made shake and by the spurs pluck'd up
The pine and cedar: graves at my command
Have waked their sleepers, oped, and let 'em forth
By my so potent art. But this rough magic
I here abjure, and, when I have required
Some heavenly music, which even now I do,
To work mine end upon their senses that
This airy charm is for, I'll break my staff,
Bury it certain fathoms in the earth,
And deeper than did ever plummet sound
I'll drown my book.

The pupil below was asked to comment on how this scene could be performed. Read through their thoughts, decide whether you would use their suggestion and add some of your own

Challenge 25

	Worth considering? **Green** Yes **Amber** Not sure (a bit hesitant) **Red** No	How else could you explore the use of ...
Prospero's magic robes could be tattered and old at this stage in the play to reflect that he no longer needs them to exist and find peace within himself.		costume
Light could be beginning to shine increasingly brightly through the robes to show that Prospero has himself, seen the light in his journey from vengeance to reconciliation.		light
The actor playing Prospero should be informed of the huge significance of him deciding to renounce his magic powers – this should be emphasised through the reflective and melancholy body language of Prospero who should appear languid at times and a mixture of sadness and imminent release.		body language
At the point when Prospero comments that if Ariel has feelings then so should he, the audience should be able to see this as a cathartic moment for Prospero, perhaps revealed through an increasing intensity of sound, a spot light and crescendo of thunder, followed by a release and outpouring of rain, symbolic of the release of anger and the welcome of reconciliation- maybe signified through a rainbow forming.		sound
As Prospero discusses his emotional journey, he could be making a physical (and psychological) line in the sand through the magic circle, which when complete would signify the story coming full circle as well as his plans coming together.		physical gestures

Sculpturing without the mess

In pairs, you need to take on the following roles:

a) Prospero

b) Sculptor

1) select your 5 favourite lines from Prospero's soliloquy

2) The sculptor (b) needs to physically position Prospero so he represents clearly the message he is trying to get across to the audience

Challenge 26

Complete the learnt section of the table you completed at the beginning of this chapter.

	Know What do I already know about this play?	Want What do I want to find out? (think about the introduction of this chapter)	Learnt What have I now learnt from this chapter that I didn't previously?
Macbeth			
Richard III			
The Tempest			
Much Ado About Nothing			

Challenge 27 - Future skills:

How might I use these skills outside of school?

As a class, you feel that it would be beneficial for you to have a trip to Shakespeare's Globe theatre though your teacher has said that there are no plans for this year.

You want to convince your head teacher that it is essential that your class goes and decide to write a persuasive letter/leaflet or speech.

Remember that you need to use your:

You may actually like the idea of a free day out in London, irrespective of Shakespeare, though you don't necessarily need to admit that in a formal piece of persuasive communication!

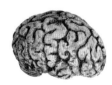 

Personalised Progression

Assessment Focus (AF3) deduce, infer or interpret information, events or ideas from texts

How is my work at KS3 assessed?

Your work is assessed using assessment focuses which help you and your teacher determine on what level your work is currently at. This criteria is often used when assessing your APP work as well as your class work and homework. In this unit we will be looking at how to progress in AF3 (see above)

Key questions:

- What level am I currently working at in this assessment focus for reading? (if unsure, ask your English teacher)
- What skills do I currently have in this assessment focus?
- What skills do I need to develop to get to the next level?

In this assessment focus (AF3), if you are currently working at…

Level 3	**go to Progress Checker A (Level 3-4 progression)**
Level 4	**go to Progress Checker B (Level 4-5 progression)**
Level 5	go to Progress Checker C (Level 5-6 progression)
Level 6	**go to Progress Checker D (Level 6-7 progression)**

When you get to the stage where you feel that you are confident in a particular level in this assessment focus, you can look at the next level to see how your work can progress.

Progress Checker A – (Level 3-4 reading progression)

	Assessment Focus (AF3) – deduce, infer or interpret information, events or ideas from texts	
1	What level am I currently working at in AF3 reading?	Level 3
2	What skills do I currently have in this assessment focus?	As a Level 3 reader in AF3 I am able to: • show meaning established at a literal level • make a straightforward comment based on a single point of reference in the text • responses based on personal speculation rather than reading of the text
3	What skills do I need to develop to reach the next level?	To be a confident AF3 reader at Level 4 I need to • make inferences based on evidence from different points in the text; • make inferences that are often correct.

Moving a Level 3 response to Level 4

The table below includes a Level 3 response in AF3. Look at how this pupil has achieved this level and think about what they could do to improve.

What can we understand about Beatrice's attitude towards men?	
AF3 – Level 3 response	**Why the pupils achieved a Level 3**
Beatrice likes Benedick and she wants him to kill Claudio. She doesn't like Claudio because he did not marry Hero. She likes some men though not others.	*Straightforward comments made* *Personal view without reference to text*

What is needed to make the next step?

AF3 – Level 3 response	**AF3 – Level 4 response**
Beatrice likes Benedick and she wants him to kill Claudio. She doesn't like Claudio because he did not marry Hero. She likes some men though not others.	*Beatrice needs Benedick in Act 4, scene I so that she can get back at Claudio "Kill Claudio" as he treated her cousin badly by saying she was with someone else. She wants to be a man herself.*

Notice how the Level 4 response makes a reference to the text itself which is a correct observation on Beatrice's attitude to men.

Progress Checker B – (Level 4-5 reading progression)

	Assessment Focus (AF3) – deduce, infer or interpret information, events or ideas from texts	
1	What level am I currently working at in AF3 reading?	Level 4
2	What skills do I currently have in this assessment focus?	As a Level 4 reader in AF3 I am able to: • make inferences based on evidence from different points in the text; • make inferences that are often correct.
3	What skills do I need to develop to reach the next level?	To be a confident AF3 reader at Level 5 I need to • develop explanation of inferred meanings by drawing on textual evidence across the text

Moving a Level 4 response to Level 5

The table below includes a Level 4 response in AF3. Look at how this pupil has achieved this level and think about what they could do to improve.

What do we discover about Macbeth's state of mind?	
AF3 – Level 4 response	**Why the pupils achieved a Level 4**
In Act 2, scene II Macbeth is frightened and feels guilty of what he has done. He refuses to go back to Duncan's room. In Act 5, scene V Macbeth is stronger and won't leave the castle	Makes correct references and inferences from different parts of the text

What is needed to make the next step?

AF3 – Level 4 response	**AF3 – Level 5 response**
In Act 2, scene II Macbeth is frightened and feels guilty of what he has done. He refuses to go back to Duncan's room. In Act 5, scene V Macbeth is stronger and won't leave the castle	Macbeth's fears are shown by the words he uses when he returns from killing Duncan. "This is a sorry sight." Later in the play he cannot be frightened anymore "I have almost forgot the taste of fear."

Notice how the Level 5 response develops an explanation from the inferences and textual evidence used.

Progress Checker C – (Level 5-6 reading progression)

	Assessment Focus (AF3) – deduce, infer or interpret information, events or ideas from texts	
1	What level am I currently working at in AF3 reading?	Level 5
2	What skills do I currently have in this assessment focus?	As a Level 5 reader in AF3 I am able to: • develop explanation of inferred meanings by drawing on textual evidence across the text
3	What skills do I need to develop to reach the next level?	To be a confident AF3 reader at Level 6 I need to • securely make comments that are based in textual evidence and identify different layers of meaning, with some attempt at detailed exploration of them, comments consider wider implications or significance of information, events or ideas in the text

Moving a Level 5 response to Level 6

The table below includes a Level 5 response in AF3. Look at how this pupil has achieved this level and think about what they could do to improve.

In these scenes, how does Richard use language to realise his ambitions?	
AF3 – Level 5 response	**Why the pupils achieved a Level 5**
The audience learn that Richard is able to use language to satisfy and realise his ruthless ambition. The way he tricks Hastings into supposedly defending Mistress Shore "Then be your eyes the witness of their evil" reveals his manipulative and cunning side; he is acutely aware of Hastings' affair with Shore's wife and takes advantage of him.	*The inferred meaning is explained in some detail, using a range of textual detail to support points made*

What is needed to make the next step?

AF3 – Level 5 response	AF3 – Level 6 response
The audience learn that Richard is able to use language to satisfy and realise his ruthless ambition. The way he tricks Hastings into supposedly defending Mistress Shore "Then be your eyes the witness of their evil" reveals his manipulative and cunning side; he is acutely aware of Hastings' affair with Shore's wife and takes advantage of him.	*Richard varies his tone and language in Act 4, Scene 2 in order to achieve his ultimate aim of ridding any barriers to his legacy. Early in the scene, he is calm and subtle in the way he questions Buckingham about whether the Princes should be killed. "Young Edward lives – think now what I would speak". Yet, when Buckingham is hesitant in his support, the tone of his language changes dramatically – it is blunt, cruel and shocking: "I wish the bastards dead!" This reveals that he is able to vary his language depending on what he wants to achieve.*

Notice how the Level 6 response begins to identify and explore the different layers of meaning

Progress Checker D – (Level 6-7 reading progression)

Assessment Focus (AF3) – deduce, infer or interpret information, events or ideas from texts

1	What level am I currently working at in AF3 reading?	Level 6
2	What skills do I currently have in this assessment focus?	As a level 6 reader in AF3 I am able to • securely make comments that are based in textual evidence and identify different layers of meaning, with some attempt at detailed exploration of them, comments consider wider implications or significance of information, events or ideas in the text
3	What skills do I need to develop to reach the next level?	To be a confident AF3 reader at Level 7 I need to • develop an interpretation of the text(s), making connections between insights, teasing out meanings or weighing up evidence.

Moving a Level 6 response to Level 7

The table below includes a Level 6 response in AF3. Look at how this pupil has achieved this level and think about what they could do to improve.

What can we deduce about the relationship between Ariel and Prospero?	
AF3 – Level 6 response	**Why the pupils achieved a Level 6**
The relationship between Prospero and Ariel is extremely complex, shown by Ariel's seeming obedience and acceptance of his role as servant "All hail, great Master"; however the reality is far different, with Ariel clearly feeling agitated and frustrated at being 'kept' by Prospero and being forced to comply with the incessant commands "Is there more toil?" *In contrast, Prospero's attitude towards his servant is clearly softer, more appreciative "I shall miss thee"* *He is also able to confide in him about whether he should forgive the men for what they have done.*	*Pupil is beginning to explore layers of meaning through the detailed analysis of their relationship and the possible reasons for the way it has developed.*

What is needed to make the next step?

AF3 – Level 6 response	AF3 – Level 7 response
The relationship between Prospero and Ariel is extremely complex, shown by Ariel's seeming obedience and acceptance of his role as servant "All hail, great Master"; however the reality is far different, with Ariel clearly feeling agitated and frustrated at being 'kept' by Prospero and being forced to comply with the incessant commands "Is there more toil?" *In contrast, Prospero's attitude towards his servant is clearly softer, more appreciative "I shall miss thee" He is also able to confide in him about whether he should forgive the men for what they have done.* 	*Shakespeare examines the relationship between Prospero and Ariel with great subtlety in these extracts, revealing that they are mutually dependent on each other for company, support, direction and ultimately release from imprisonment. Prospero's decision to release the men and Ariel from his power is a cathartic moment for him as it also allows him to be released from the emotional shackles that years of feeling a deep sense of injustice and betrayal has caused.* *In act 2, Scene 1, Ariel is shown to be cunning in the way he relates to Prospero as he is aware that his master needs constant reassurance; this, he believes hasten his own release; yet when Prospero orders more work, the true Ariel is momentarily released "Is there more toil?", as is the inner conflict that their polite exchanges have masked. When Prospero reminds his servant of how much he should be indebted to him, Ariel quickly realises that he needs to back peddle and once again reverts to archetypal servant "I thank thee master"* *Ariel's ability to manipulate the seemingly all-powerful Prospero is evident also in Act 5, Scene 1 when he manages to persuade him that he should give up his magic powers; Ariel is conscious that if this were to take place it would once again hasten his own promised release. Their need for each other emotionally is clear in these extracts, as is there inner conflict on who gains ultimate control.*

Notice how the Level 7 response begins to interpret the text, making original and insightful comments, whilst teasing out the deep layers of their relationship